D0643919

MY LIFE ON A PLATE

RECIPES FROM AROUND THE WORLD

Born and raised in Harlem, New York, Kelis Rogers, better known by just her first name, first came to prominence singing the hook of Ol' Dirty Bastard's hit Got Your Money. Years of chart dominating songs and thrilling, boundary-pushing music followed resulting in millions of albums sold and numerous top 10 hits. She has released six albums, won Brit, Q, and NME Awards, and been nominated for two Grammy Awards. Her latest album Food, made with a live band and horn section, mints a sound that is rootsy, raw, and soulful without ever being retro. Upon release the album was praised as one of her most adventurous works yet. Kelis has toured every corner of the world, performed at every major festival, and shared the stage with the world's top artists. A fashion icon and designer muse since the early days of her career, she is celebrated for a personal style which is often as creative and forward-thinking as the music she makes. Besides her career in music, Kelis is a Le Cordon Bleu-trained chef with multiple television cooking specials, and a burgeoning entrepreneurial streak with her Bounty & Full organic sauce line.
www.bountyandfull.com

This book is for you, Mom.
Thank you for endlessly pouring into me. I'm proud to be your daughter.

To Knight, I want to leave with you an abundance of wonderful things, so this too is for you. I love you.

MY LIFE ON A PLATE

RECIPES FROM AROUND THE WORLD

Kelis

with Carolynn Carreño

Photography **David Loftus**
Illustrations **Hannah Morrison**

KYLE BOOKS

Published in 2015 by Kyle Books
www.kylebooks.com

Distributed by National Book Network
4501 Forbes Blvd, Suite 200,
Lanham, MD 20706
Phone: (800) 462-6420
Fax: (800) 338-4550
customercare@nbnbooks.com

10 9 8 7 6 5 4 3 2 1

ISBN 978-1-909487-30-7

Editor: Kyle Cathie
Editorial Assistant: Claire Rogers
Copy Editor: Sarah Scheffel
Designer: Anita Mangan
Photographer: David Loftus
Illustrator: Hannah Morrison
Food Stylists: Sophia Green,
assisted by Sarah Asch & Jessica Vliet
Prop Stylist: Robin Turk
Hair: Maisha Oliver
Make up: Gaby Torell
Production: Nic Jones, Gemma John,
and Lisa Pinnell
Management for Kelis: Steve Satterthwaite, Geoff Barnett,
and Alexis Peluso for Red Light Management

Library of Congress Control Number: 2013952643
Color reproduction by ALTA London
Printed and bound in Slovenia by DZS

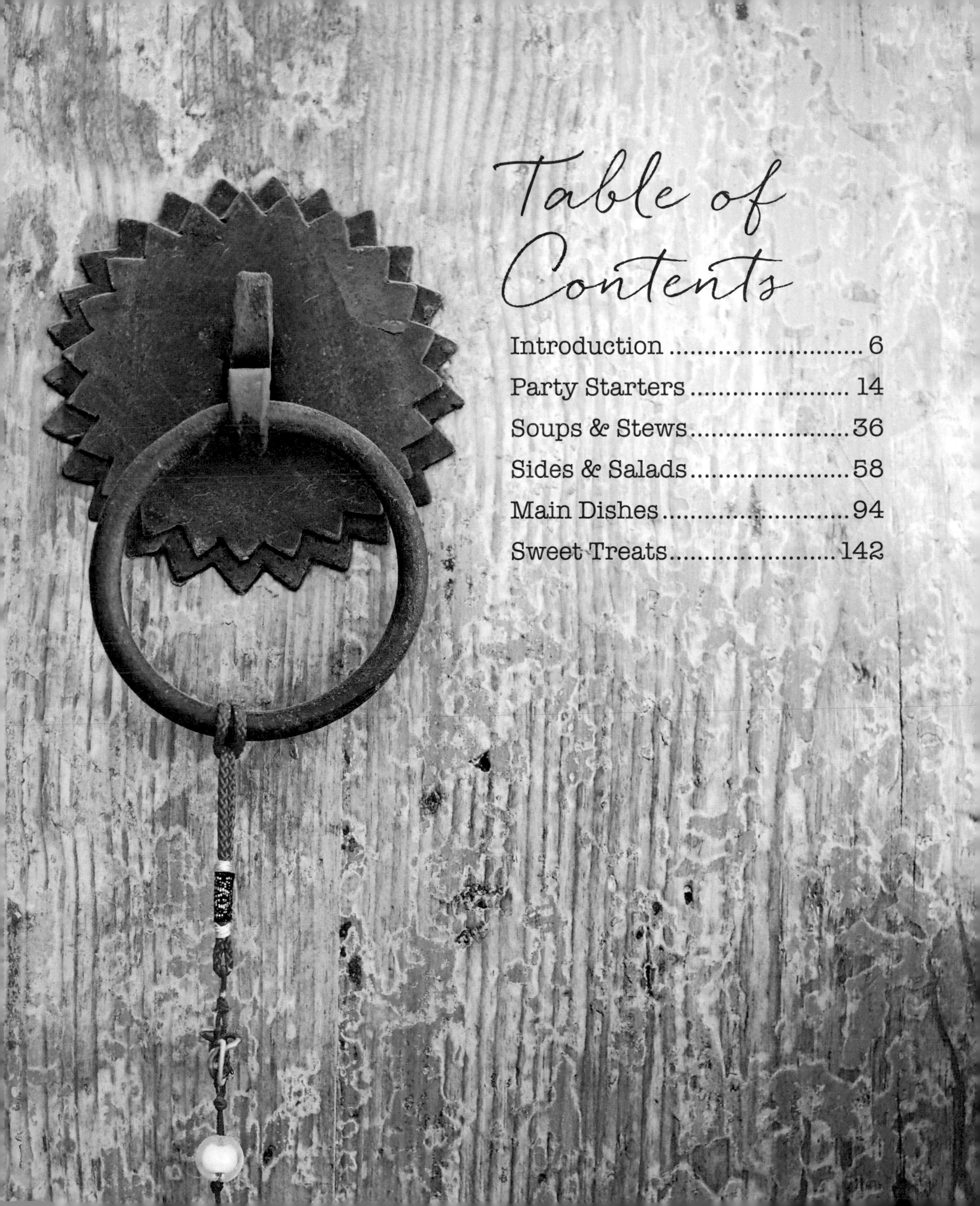

Table of Contents

"Take it all in & kiss it up to the sky"

Bounty & Full

I am my mother's daughter. I can't really say when my love affair with food actually started. I don't even really remember learning to cook. I don't remember learning to sing either for that matter. But I do remember watching her cook. Every detail was clear and defined. Red lips, red nails, perfume, earrings, and a military demeanor that she wore like a royal garment. She was the first chef I'd ever met. When I was growing up she had her own catering and event planning business. There was nothing she couldn't do. I was in the presence of a master. She had a hard working staff but I was always there. I would do anything she asked or she'd let me. I loved the speed, the intensity in the kitchen, the burn, and all the hustle and bustle of flowers and platters buzzing by. Not one detail was ever left out. Nothing was ever served at the wrong temperature and it was all always beautiful.

I was born in NY: a native New Yorker and the daughter of a musician and a chef. Get it now? We are what we breathe and eat. At least I am. If you've ever been to my city you'll know that there's barely room enough for everything. But that's why we're so loud. And the food says it all. Little Italy has been reduced to about 2 city blocks of late, but it sits nestled right next to Chinatown. On Sundays after church, sometimes my family would go downtown to Theresa's on Eleventh and First for perogies and kielbasa. I didn't care much then, but I'd eaten my way around the world by the age of eleven on the tiny island of Manhattan. And what a small world it is after all.

I attended LaGuardia High School, better-known back then as the *Fame* school, in the 90s when people were cool and parties were fun. After the club I'd sneak into, we'd go to Third and McDougal for shawarma and falafels at Mamouns, a perfect 3 a.m. snack. I graduated and, before I could even think about my next step, I was signed to Virgin Records for my first album. I went everywhere. I was performing in places I had never even heard of. I was shopping in markets that really were hidden treasures and the food, my friend, the food! It was right before the gentrification of the world, so I've watched it change. Let me explain, though. There was no McDonald's on the Champs Elysées in Paris, and street food in Bangkok was not considered trendy or cool but dangerous and a death wish. Those were the good old days. Traveling still held a sense of prestige and awe. Crossing paths with so many artists and bands along the way, the no-name club in any particular city in any particular country became our Vegas. What happens in (insert anywhere) stays... there. Too young to notice, too stupid to care.

I woke up one morning and ten years had just happened. Just like that. I wasn't strung out or wallowing in self-pity, but it suddenly occurred to me that this was all I had done, and that, even though I recognized it as a blessing, I thought it wise to get off the train for a moment and gain some perspective. It also just so happened that I was, for the first time since I was seventeen, truly a free agent. I wasn't signed and I had no obligations to anyone. Plus, by that point I was habitually irritated and bored with the industry that had raised me.

This story is coming to its point, right now. So here it is: I was sitting in my house in Silver Lake, California at the kitchen counter on Friday afternoon, and I heard a commercial on TV for a culinary school. And like a cartoon anvil had just been released from the sky, I was hit. Yes, my most brilliant idea yet! That's what I'm going to do next. I'll never forget, I looked up the number for Le Cordon Bleu and within a few minutes it was

decided that I would start the semester full-time bright and early Monday morning.

It is rare that I say this about anything, but as soon as I hung up the phone I was terrified and so nervous: first day of school jitters but on steroids. I was too old for this, and I hadn't had a boss in more than 10 years. Hell, I had just declared how bossy I was to the world with ring tones ricocheting in assorted pre-teen gatherings across this great nation. I certainly had not been in a class setting in even longer than that. So, yes, I was in awe of what I'd done. I wasn't even sure if my brain was still equipped to learn any real valuable information. I thought for sure I had left those brain cells in an ashtray in Istanbul or anywhere many moons ago.

I won't ramble on with any more details about that, but I gotta tell you that something, no, everything changed. I was enthralled. I soon realized that, fear aside, this was one of the best things I would ever do. I wasn't a mother yet so this held steady in its position for a while.

I have always loved talking to the elderly, the ones who are lucid and can keep their story straight, but, more seriously, because it reminds me that it's not over till it's over. And that whether I went on to write my greatest album yet, or never stood behind a Neumann U87 again, this was just another chapter, and I didn't owe anyone any explanations for running away into the arms of a big, fat kitchen. I was good here. I loved that.

So, blah, blah, blah, and on and on. I did release another album and I went on tour. I started talking pictures of the markets, and slipped away to food adventures when there was no gig, literally eating my way from sea to sea. I've always had a bit of an issue with punctuality, but that was those days and for different reasons we won't speak of here. Then, I was showing up at shows just in the nick of time, and I was so full. The last thing I wanted was to squeeze into that sequined catsuit. You can't even imagine—there were so many days like that. I was more in the mood for a nap. But that's beside the point. The point is that I love finding the tiniest hole in the wall with the best roti tisu on the southern coast of Penang.

I started taking gigs in cities that made no sense career-wise for my music, but because it was my little secret: I was basically going for a food tour from country to country, often day to day. I had to learn how to detect quickly what was important and what was valuable in each place I visited, so that time was not wasted. It was like developing my own Cliff's Notes or synopsis. Ironically, music and food are the quickest and most surefire ways to do that. Tell me what you eat and what you listen to, and I'll tell you who you are. What began happening was that I was taking so many crash courses on each city's food that, naturally, I started to make comparisons and see similarities. What I realized is that, while I may not have been fully focused in Dr. Schneider's history class fifth period, he might have been on to something. You can trace our history through food and cooking techniques if you look closely. We can see where

something originated and how it got here, and, for all of our differences, wars and religions, we all started off with the same ideas. There is no real departure between gyoza and empanadas, perogies and samosas. Who doesn't love a whole roasted pig? That crispy skin that you hear crunch and crackle... there's no vegan substitute. And rice stained with the vibrant color of saffron in Spain (where I had the pleasure to live for the better part of a year) is so similar to the achiote in Puerto Rico where I spent every summer with my family as a child. The food I'm drawn to is the food that tells us who we are and what we are. It can have personality, heartache, and rebirth all on one plate. What better way to tell our story? This is who I am. This is who we are.

I remember, during my first trip to Beirut, being at the house of a friend's friend who had a friend and how I was welcomed into his home and the spread of food completely covered the table. We were planning our day's drive to see the cedars and suddenly I lost what I was planning to say, because, though the words were right there at the tip of my tongue about to trickle out with ease, on its way into my mouth was my first encounter with biryani Saudi-style. Between the heat, the precision of the rice, and the temperature on the patio that night, it was clear I had just met the star of the show. Pleasure to meet you. And, although out of respect it was not appropriate to enjoy a glass of wine at this particular dinner, it didn't stop me from salivating at the memory of my Australian summer and my first introduction into big reds and how perfect, under different circumstances, a full-bodied Shiraz would be with flavors like this.

I can go on and on, and I will as we progress. I want this book to represent life lived casually and abundantly. I have no delusions, there's no reason to recreate the wheel, and I wouldn't dare suggest that I could. However, over the past 15 years, I've been swindled and enchanted by some of what I think are the most tantalizing and yet obvious flavors in the world, and, if I've learned anything from the experiences, it's that the very nature of who we are probably started somewhere, some time, long ago at the bottom of an ancient cast iron skillet much like mine.

Living well. Eating well. Being well is a lifestyle. I believe if we treat our everyday with the same consistency of thought our quality of life is elevated. It doesn't have to be a task; it shouldn't be. I made a list that's ongoing, of things I keep in my home and pantry. So cooking is fun and can be spontaneous.

Here's a list for your start up kitchen. You may already have a lot of these things. It's easy to interchange and play around with recipes once your foundation is laid. You should replenish as you go along but your pantry and kitchen should never be empty. These are just some basics but think about your eating habits and what flavors feel like home to you and add to the list to make it your own. Have fun and buen provecho!

Equipment

- Food processor (it can be small but a chef's must-have)
- Chef knife
- Cast iron skillet
- A few wooden spoons
- Cutting board
- Blender
- Measuring cups
- Potato peeler
- Cheese grater

Dairy

- Butter
- Sour cream
- Milk
- Heavy whipping cream
- Yogurt

In the cupboard

- Canned coconut milk
- Condensed milk
- Evaporated milk
- Sugar
- All purpose flour
- Baking powder
- Baking soda
- Vanilla extract
- Kosher salt (my preference)
- Granulated garlic
- Paprika
- Cinnamon
- Nutmeg
- Cayenne
- Dried herbs (oregano, thyme, rosemary , basil)
- Curry powder
- Black pepper (I like to grind my own. I use a coffee grinder)
- Bag of brown rice (what I like but it can be any white rice if you prefer. I also always keep some barley and quinoa in my pantry)
- Coarse cornmeal
- Rolled dried oats
- Whole grain flour

Fruit & Vegetables

- Onions
- Garlic
- Bell peppers, red and green
- Frozen corn
- Frozen fruit (whatever you like)
- Stock (vegetable and chicken, you can make your own and store it or buy it. If you buy it make sure it's low sodium)
- Beans (dried or canned)
- Chickpeas
- Crushed tomatoes
- Tomato sauce (these 2 ingredients are just good for back up)

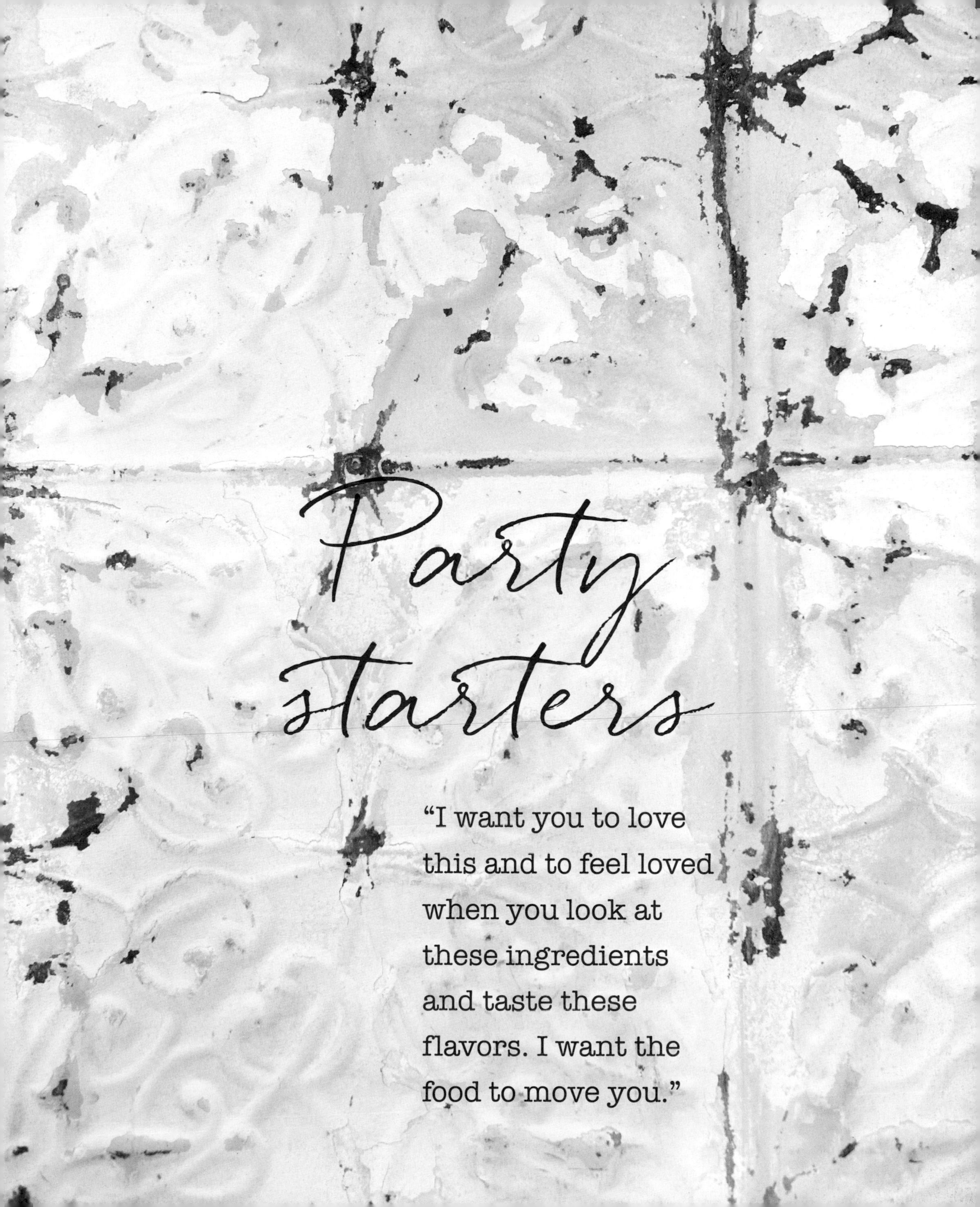

Party starters

"I want you to love this and to feel loved when you look at these ingredients and taste these flavors. I want the food to move you."

Spinach & Feta Pinwheels

These are spinach pies. They are great for dinner parties. I like to serve them with some wine while I put the finishing touches on the rest of the meal.

MAKES 16 PINWHEELS

- 2½ tablespoons olive oil
- ½ yellow onion, finely chopped
- 1¾ teaspoons kosher salt
- 5 garlic cloves, minced
- 6 loosely packed cups fresh spinach leaves
- 1 tablespoon balsamic vinegar
- 1 large egg
- 1 teaspoon black pepper
- ½ cup crumbled feta
- All-purpose flour for dusting
- 1 (1-pound) package frozen phyllo dough, thawed according to the package instructions
- ½ cup (1 stick) unsalted butter, melted
- 1 large egg whisked with 1 tablespoon water for the egg wash

1. Heat the oil in a medium saucepan on medium-low heat. Add the chopped onion, sprinkle with ¾ teaspoon of the salt, and cook gently, stirring often, until the onion is tender and translucent, about 10 minutes. Toss in the garlic and cook for 1 minute, stirring constantly so it doesn't burn. Add the spinach and vinegar, season with ½ teaspoon of the salt, and cook until the spinach is wilted, about 2 minutes, folding the spinach as it wilts. Drain the spinach mixture through a colander and push on it gently with the back of a spoon to strain out the excess water. Set aside to cool to room temperature.
2. Whisk the egg, pepper, and the remaining ½ teaspoon salt in a large bowl. Add the spinach mixture and stir to combine. Gently fold in the feta.
3. Position an oven rack in the center and preheat the oven to 350°F.
4. Dust a flat work surface lightly with flour and lay down 1 sheet of phyllo. Brush the phyllo with some of the melted butter and lay another sheet on top of it. Brush with more butter and continue until you have stacked 10 sheets of dough; do not brush the top sheet with butter. Using a dough scraper and rolling pastry cutter or knife, cut the stacked phyllo into 2-inch squares. Working with 1 square of dough at a time, make a ¾-inch cut at a 45-degree angle to each of the four corners. Spoon a heaping tablespoon of the spinach filling in the center of each square of dough. Fold every other corner inward, creating a pinwheel shape. Brush the exposed dough with the egg wash and place the pinwheel on an ungreased baking sheet. Repeat with the remaining squares of dough, then repeat again with the remaining 10 sheets of phyllo dough.
5. Bake the pinwheels on the center rack for 5 to 7 minutes, until they are golden brown.

Chickpea Hummus

I live in an area of Los Angeles that has a large population of people from the Middle East and Israel, and hummus is sold in stores and restaurants all over the neighborhood. Living there, I fell in love with it and now hummus feels like my native cuisine. I make hummus often because it's easy to throw together and it feels like a healthy snack for me and my family. I like to serve it with a really beautiful plate of vegetables, including sliced tomatoes, celery, carrots, cucumbers, and any other delicious vegetables I might have around.

MAKES ABOUT 3 CUPS

2 (15-ounce) cans garbanzo beans, drained

¼ yellow onion, roughly chopped

4 garlic cloves, peeled

¾ cup olive oil

3 tablespoons fresh lemon juice

1½ tablespoons Dijon mustard

½ teaspoon black pepper

½ teaspoon ground cumin

3 teaspoons kosher salt, plus more to taste

1. Put all of the ingredients in the bowl of a food processor fitted with a metal blade and... viola! A delicious and healthy snack! Add more salt to taste.

Black Bean Hummus

I make a bunch of different flavors of hummus, but besides the classic, black bean is my favorite. It's well worth the little amount of time it takes to make your own hummus. Whenever I buy it ready-made instead, I get home and taste it and it's never as flavorful as one I whip together myself.

MAKES ABOUT 4 CUPS

2 (15-ounce) cans garbanzo beans, drained

1 (15-ounce) can black beans, drained

½ cup olive oil

4 garlic cloves, peeled

1 jalapeño pepper, seeded and roughly chopped

2 tablespoons fresh lime juice

2½ teaspoons kosher salt, plus more to taste

½ teaspoon black pepper

1. Put all of the ingredients in the bowl of a food processor fitted with a metal blade and purée. Add more salt to taste.

Shrimp Alcapurrias

When I was growing up, we spent every summer with family in Puerto Rico. There's an area there by the sea called Piñones where they sell little snacks, all made with seafood, including shrimp alcapurrias. These deep-fried, stuffed grated yucca (some people also make them with green plantains) are amazing and remind me of who I am. And can be filled with meat or seafood.

When graduating from culinary school, for the last project of our chef dissertation, they gave us an ingredient, and with that one ingredient we had to make something in the French style that we'd learned in school… My ingredient was yucca, so I called my mom to ask her how to make alcapurrias. She called my grandmother, who said I wouldn't be able to do them because I didn't have the traditional banana leaves to roll the balls in. She said how tedious it was—I think she didn't want me to make them, or to fail making them. It makes me laugh now. I'm like, "Geez, thanks for the vote of confidence, Mom." I think my grandmother made them so well that my mom figured there was just no use in trying. I decided to do it anyway. All the women in my family were holding their breath, thinking I was going to fail, but the alcapurrias were easy enough to roll in my hands. And they turned out really amazing! The chewy crunchiness of the yucca is unusual and the spicy, flavorful shrimp filling is so good. I got an A-plus.

You will have more filling than you need for these; you can use it on top of Smoked Bacon Arepas (page 22), scramble it in eggs, or serve it over brown rice.

MAKES 16 TO 20 PIECES

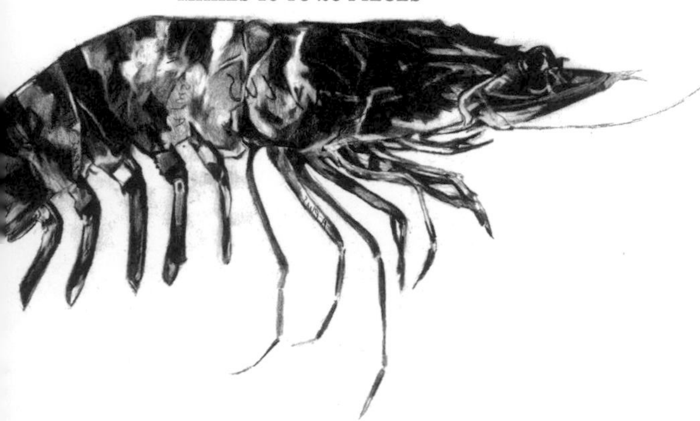

For the yucca coating

2 yucca, peeled and shredded on a box grater using the microplane side (about 4 cups)

2 tablespoons Sofrito (page 75)

1 tablespoon Sazón (page 21) or 1 teaspoon achiote paste plus 1 tablespoon kosher salt, crumbled with your fingers

½ teaspoon black pepper

For the shrimp filling

2 tablespoons olive oil

½ large yellow onion, minced

1 teaspoon kosher salt

6 garlic cloves, minced

½ green bell pepper, cored, seeded, and minced

½ red bell pepper, cored, seeded, and minced

¼ cup Sofrito

1 teaspoon dried oregano

½ teaspoon ground cumin

½ teaspoon black pepper

½ teaspoon cayenne pepper

½ teaspoon achiote paste, crumbled with your fingers

1¼ pounds shrimp, peeled, deveined, and minced

Canola or vegetable oil for deep frying

1 cup all-purpose flour

1. To prepare the yucca, put the yucca in a piece of doubled-up cheesecloth and squeeze to strain out the excess liquid. Transfer to a large bowl, cover, and refrigerate for several hours. Strain the yucca again to extract excess liquid. Season with the sofrito, Sazón or achiote paste, and pepper, and mix to blend the flavors.
2. Meanwhile, make the shrimp filling. Heat the oil in a large sauté pan over medium-high heat. Add the onion, season with half the salt, and sauté for about 5 minutes, until the onion begins to soften. Toss in the garlic and peppers, and sauté for about 5 minutes to soften. Add the sofrito, oregano, cumin, black pepper,

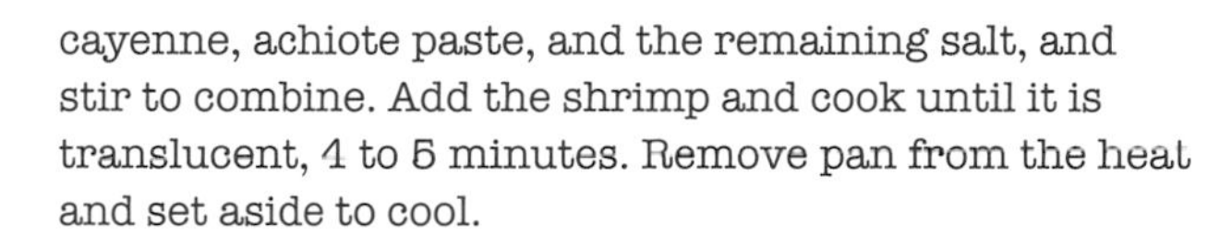

cayenne, achiote paste, and the remaining salt, and stir to combine. Add the shrimp and cook until it is translucent, 4 to 5 minutes. Remove pan from the heat and set aside to cool.

3. When you're ready to fry the alcapurrias, heat 3 to 4 inches of oil in a large saucepan over medium heat until the oil reaches 350°F. Strain the yucca mixture through a double layer of cheesecloth again, extracting as much liquid as possible. Prepare a bed of paper towels for draining.

4. Put the flour into a shallow bowl. Scoop ¼ cup of the yucca mixture and form it into a patty in your palms. Put about 2 teaspoons of the shrimp filling in the center and close the patty to make a tiny football shape. Coat the ball in the flour. Repeat until you have used all of the yucca or filling. Slide the alcapurrias into the hot oil and deep-fry until they are golden brown and cooked through, 6 to 8 minutes. Remove from the oil and drain on paper towels. Serve immediately.

Sazón

Sazón, which means seasoning in Spanish, is one of a range of seasoning mixes made by Goya, a brand of Latino foods, which is a key ingredient in our cooking. Achiote is a paste made from annatto seeds. It's what gives our rice its pretty yellow color. It's hard to make Puerto Rican food without Sazón. The Goya version is readily available in New York and Los Angeles and anywhere else that there are large populations of Latin people, but if you can't get it, you can make your own using this recipe. You can use achiote or tumeric.

MAKES ABOUT 2 CUPS

¼ cup plus 3 tablespoons granulated onion

⅓ cup granulated garlic

⅓ cup dried oregano

¼ cup smoked paprika

3 tablespoons plus 1 teaspoon ground coriander

3 tablespoons ground cumin

2 tablespoons plus 1 teaspoon kosher salt

1 tablespoon plus 1 teaspoon black pepper

2 teaspoons ground turmeric

1. Pulse all of the ingredients together in a food processor fitted with a metal blade. Store at room temperature in a jar with a tight-fitting lid for up to 3 months.

Smoked Bacon Arepas

Many Central and South American cultures make arepas, but these are Colombian. My husband is Colombian, and when we first started dating, he was like, "I'm going to come over and make you something." He made it seem like it was this really spectacular culinary extravaganza, which is very cute, because actually it's the easiest thing in the world! And really delicious. As a consequence, I fell in love with arepas, and I fell in love with him. Colombian arepas are really thin, so they aren't cut in half like a lot of arepas are. I like bacon in my dough but you can also use scallions or corn too. Arepas have been completely integrated into our family cuisine, which is nice. I make a bunch of them and then throw one in the toaster for a snack for my son. You can top them with all kinds of stuff: white cheese, Ají (page 45), avocado, soft chorizo, a fried or scrambled egg. Asking me what you can put on an arepa is like asking someone what you can put on bread…

Traditionally, Colombian arepas are cooked on a grill but I also give you directions for cooking them in a skillet, which is more convenient.

INGREDIENT NOTE: Harina Venezolana is a specialty Colombian product which you can get from a specialty market or the internet.

MAKES 12 AREPAS

3 cups masa harina Venezolana (precooked white cornmeal), or any other precooked masa harina

½ teaspoon truffle salt

7 cups boiling water

7 ounces bacon slices, pan-fried and chopped

2 tablespoons canola oil, or more as needed (if you're cooking the arepas in a skillet)

¾ pound queso cotija, crumbled (you can substitute feta or Spanish white cheese)

1. Put the masa and the salt in a large bowl. Slowly pour in the boiling water, mixing with a wooden spoon to form a dough. Knead the dough a few times while it's still in the bowl to form a ball.
2. Scoop up ¼ cup of the dough (about 2½ ounces), press in some of the bacon, and shape it into a disc that's about ½ inch thick and 3 inches across.
3. Preheat a grill to medium-low heat, or heat the oil in a skillet over medium-low heat. Grill the arepas or cook them in the skillet until golden brown, 6 to 8 minutes per side, turning them only once.
4. Crumble the cheese and whatever topping you are putting on the arepas. Sprinkle with a little salt depending on choice of topping, and serve.

Spinach & Chickpea Fritters with Yogurt Cucumber Sauce

When I was in high school, friends and I used to go at three in the morning to a little hole in the wall called Mamoun's Falafel in the Village for falafel pitas and I've been hooked on falafel ever since. These fritters are inspired by falafels but they're lighter and fluffier. They're smaller than traditional falafel, about the size of ping pong balls.

MAKES ABOUT 4 DOZEN FRITTERS

2 (15-ounce) cans chickpeas, drained

1 loosely packed cup fresh spinach leaves

¼ large yellow onion, roughly chopped

3 tablespoons all-purpose flour

3 garlic cloves, smashed and chopped

1 fresh dill sprig, roughly chopped

1½ teaspoons kosher salt

½ teaspoon black pepper

¼ teaspoon ground sage

¼ teaspoon ground coriander

Canola or vegetable oil for deep-frying

1 recipe Yogurt Cucumber Sauce (see below)

1. Place all the ingredients in the bowl of a food processor fitted with a metal blade, and purée to create a smooth batter, then transfer to a mixing bowl.
2. In a medium saucepan, heat 3 to 4 inches of oil over medium heat until the oil reaches 350°F. Prepare a bed of paper towels for draining the fritters.
3. Spoon out 1 tablespoon of batter, shape it into a ball with your hands, and then flatten it to make a little disc. Drop the disc into the oil and continue to shape and add more little discs of batter to the pan, frying each fritter until golden brown, about 5 minutes. Remove each from the oil when it is done, transferring it to the paper towels to drain, and continuing to shape and add more discs to the pan. When all of the fritters are fried, sprinkle them with salt. Serve warm, with the yogurt sauce on the side.

Yogurt Cucumber Sauce

I served this for a lunch feast at home in Los Angeles. It was actually a business meeting, but I figured: Since we were all together, let's make a day of it. I was thinking summer in the Mediterranean, so I made Spinach and Chickpea Fritters (see above), whole baked branzino, tomatoes, and this yogurt sauce. The sauce was meant specifically for dipping the fritters, but it went with everything on the table. You can serve the sauce with grilled lamb, or use it to make sandwiches on fresh-from-the-oven pita bread that I buy in my neighborhood.

MAKES ABOUT 2 CUPS

1½ cups plain Greek yogurt

¼ cup finely chopped cucumber

2 tablespoons minced yellow onion

2 garlic cloves, minced

1 tablespoon fresh lemon juice

1 teaspoon kosher salt

1. In a medium bowl, stir all of the ingredients together until thoroughly combined. Cover and refrigerate until ready to serve.

Japanese Yam Samosas

One of the things I love about traveling is connecting the dots in terms of how different cultures eat. What I've learned is that people are all the same and we all want to eat the same things. Deep-fried dough is one of those universal things. Stuffed with meat or potato or veggies, whether you call them samosas, pirogies, gyoza, ponchiks, empanadas or dumplings, they're delicious.

I was working in Singapore, staying at the Marina Bay Sandy Hotel, and underneath the rest of the building is the mother load of food courts. It's magnificent! There I had this incredible chutney-flavored, doughy-textured dumpling. We did not speak the same language, but what joy that dumpling brought me. It was a perfect sweet Japanese yam. These samosas remind me of that day.

MAKES 32 SAMOSAS

1 teaspoon kosher salt plus more for boiling and seasoning

2 pounds Japanese (yellow-fleshed) yams, peeled and cut into large chunks

2 carrots, peeled and cut into a small dice

2 teaspoons curry powder

½ teaspoon ground cumin

½ teaspoon ground coriander

½ cup frozen petit peas, thawed

1 recipe Buttery Flakey Everything Dough (page 157)

Canola or vegetable oil for deep-frying

1. Bring a large pot of water to a boil and salt it to taste like the ocean. Add the yams and boil until tender, about 15 minutes. Put the carrots in a strainer and, 1 minute before the yams are done, dunk the strainer into the water to blanch the carrots. Remove the strainer and set aside. Drain the yams in a colander, transfer them to a large bowl, and mash the yams with a potato masher. Add the curry powder, cumin, coriander, and salt and mash to distribute the seasonings. Fold in the carrots and peas. Season with more salt to taste.
2. Divide the dough into 16 equal-size (about 1½ ounce) balls. Roll each ball out to create a square about 4 inches across and ⅛ inch thick. Fold one corner over the middle and fold the second corner over so that the edges meet. Pinch to seal the edges, creating a round cone with the top open. Spoon 1 heaping tablespoon of the filling into the cone and pinch to close. Put the samosa aside and continue shaping and filling the remaining samosas until you have used up all of the dough and filling.
3. In a large saucepan, heat 3 inches of oil over medium heat until the oil reaches 350°F. Prepare a bed of paper towels for draining the samosas.
4. When the oil is hot, put as many samosas in the oil as will fit comfortably and fry for 6 to 8 minutes, turning to cook evenly, until golden brown and crispy. Remove the samosas from the oil and drain them on the paper towels. Let the oil return to 350°F, then fry the remaining samosas in the same way. Serve immediately.

Papas Rellenas

Papas rellenas, which means 'stuffed potatoes', are most popular in Peru, Chile, Cuba, Columbia, and of course Puerto Rico. They are potato balls filled with picadillo, a seasoned ground meat mixture, and then deep fried. When I see papas rellenas in New York, they're huge, like softballs. In LA, they're tiny, like golf balls. Who knows why the difference; I make mine about the size of a tennis ball. You can serve these as an appetizer or a meal; two or three would be a great dinner. You'll have picadillo leftover after making the papas rellenas. Serve it on top of brown rice, bulgur wheat, or mashed potatoes.

MAKES 12 PIECES; 4 CUPS MEAT FILLING TOTAL

For the picadillo

2 tablespoons olive oil

3 tablespoons Sofrito (page 75)

1 large yellow onion, minced

3 teaspoons kosher salt

1 teaspoon ground black pepper

2 garlic cloves, finely chopped

1 large heirloom or vine-ripened tomato, diced

2 pounds ground beef

1½ tablespoons smoked paprika

1½ teaspoons dried oregano

1 teaspoon ground cumin

¼ cup whole small pimento-stuffed olives, cut in half

For the potatoes

1 pound Yukon gold potatoes, peeled and cut into large chunks

Kosher salt for the boiling water

1½ cups club soda

1 cup all-purpose flour

Canola or vegetable oil for deep-frying

1. To make the picadillo, heat the oil in a large (preferably cast iron) skillet over medium-high heat. Add the sofrito and cook it for 1 minute. Add the onion and season with 1 teaspoon of the salt and ½ teaspoon of the pepper. Reduce the heat to medium and cook, stirring often, until the onion is tender and translucent, about 10 minutes. Scatter the garlic into the pan and cook for about 1 minute, until it's fragrant, stirring so it doesn't brown. Add the tomato and its juices and cook for 3 or 4 minutes, until it begins to break down. Add the ground beef and break it into small pieces with a wooden spoon. Sprinkle with the paprika, oregano, cumin, the remaining 2 teaspoons of salt and ½ teaspoon pepper. Cook until the meat is no longer pink, stirring often, about 5 minutes. Stir in the olives and cook for about 2 minutes to meld the flavors. Set aside to cool to room temperature.
2. To prepare the potatoes, bring a large pot of water to a boil and salt it to taste like the ocean. Add the potatoes and cook until they are tender and crumbly but not mush, about 20 minutes. Drain the potatoes in a colander and transfer them to a large bowl. Smash them with a potato masher to crumble but not completely mash them. Put them in the refrigerator to cool to room temperature. (Cooling them helps the papas rellenas stay crispy and whole when fried.)
3. Scoop up ¼ cup of the potato mixture and make a potato patty as thin as you can with your hands. Put 1 heaping tablespoon of the picadillo in the center of the patty and roll the potato around it to form a round about the size of a tennis ball. Put the ball on a baking sheet and continue rolling more balls until you have used all of the potatoes.
4. Combine the club soda and flour in a medium bowl and whisk to break up any lumps to make a batter.
5. In a large saucepan, heat 3 to 4 inches of oil over medium heat until the oil reaches 350°F.
6. One at a time, dip half of the papas rellenas in the batter and carefully drop them into the oil. Fry for 4 to 5 minutes, until golden brown and crispy. Use a slotted spoon to remove, and place them on paper towels to drain. Repeat with the remaining papas. Serve warm.

Shredded Beef Sliders with Root Beer Espresso BBQ Sauce

I started making these when I had a food truck at South by Southwest music and film festival in Austin, Texas, to showcase my new line of sauces. The meat is a version of ropa vieja, or "old clothes," which is braised, shredded flank steak traditional to many cuisines of the Caribbean. My mom makes ropa vieja all the time; I learned to make it from her. To utilize my barbecue sauce, I got the idea to toss ropa vieja with the sauce and then use the meat to make sliders. You can also serve the meat (with or without sauce) with rice, which is how Puerto Ricans traditionally eat ropa vieja, or use it to fill pastelitos, which is the Puerto Rican version of empanadas, or meat pies, using Buttery Flakey Everything Dough (page 157) for the pie shells. It's good too with rice or leftover mashed potato. You can use Bounty & Full Wild Cherry BBQ sauce for this, which is how this dish originated.

MAKES 4 CUPS OR ENOUGH FOR 16 SLIDERS

6 fresh thyme sprigs

4 fresh oregano sprigs

2 fresh rosemary sprigs

2 pounds flank steak, cut into 2 segments to fit in your pan

1 tablespoon kosher salt, plus more to taste

¾ teaspoon coarse ground black pepper

2 tablespoons olive oil

2 medium yellow onions, coarsely chopped

1 green and 1 red bell pepper, cored, seeded, and coarsely chopped

15 cloves garlic, peeled

1 teaspoon smoked paprika

½ teaspoon ground cumin

½ cup Root Beer Espresso BBQ Sauce (page 33), or use store-bought

16 small brioche buns, cut in half

½ cup (1 stick) unsalted butter, melted

1. Wrap the thyme, oregano, and rosemary in a doubled piece of cheesecloth and tie it closed with kitchen string to make an herb bouquet.
2. Season the meat on both sides with the salt and pepper.
3. Heat the oil in a large soup pot or Dutch oven over medium-high heat for about 3 minutes, until it's searing hot. Add 1 piece of meat to the pot and sear it until it is deep brown on both sides, 5 to 7 minutes per side. Remove the meat from the pan and sear the second piece of meat. Leave the second one in the pot and return the first piece, too. Add the herb bouquet, onions, green and red bell peppers, garlic, paprika, cumin and enough water to just cover the meat and vegetables. Bring the water to a boil over high heat, reduce the heat to low, cover the pot, and simmer until the meat can be gently torn apart with a fork, about 2 hours. Turn off the heat and let the meat cool to room temperature in the liquid.
4. Lift the meat out of the liquid and shred it back into the pot with the cooking liquid. (I like to go at it with kitchen shears.) Remove the herb bouquet and stir in the barbecue sauce. Season with salt to taste.
5. Brush the insides of the buns with the melted butter and toast the insides only under the broiler. Scoop ¼ cup of the barbecue beef onto each bun and serve.

Root Beer Espresso BBQ Sauce

MAKES ABOUT 3 CUPS

2 tablespoons olive oil
1 yellow onion, roughly chopped
4 teaspoons kosher salt, plus a pinch of salt (or more to taste)
8 garlic cloves, roughly chopped
¼ cup distilled white vinegar
2 vine-ripened tomatoes, chopped
1 cup canned or bottled tomato sauce
½ cup yellow mustard
1 packed cup light or dark brown sugar
¾ cup root beer
2 tablespoons balsamic vinegar
2 tablespoons molasses
2 teaspoons pure vanilla extract
3 tablespoons honey
1 tablespoon finely ground espresso
1 teaspoon black pepper, plus more to taste
1 teaspoon ground paprika
1 teaspoon chili powder
½ teaspoon cayenne pepper
½ teaspoon ground allspice
¾ teaspoon garlic powder
½ teaspoon ground cumin

1. Combine the oil and onion in a large saucepan over medium-low heat.
2. Sprinkle with 1 teaspoon of the salt and cook about 10 minutes, until the onion is tender and translucent, stirring often so the onion doesn't brown.
3. Add the garlic and a pinch of salt and sauté for 1 to 2 minutes, until the garlic is fragrant, stirring constantly so it doesn't brown.
4. Add the white vinegar, increase the heat to medium-high, and cook for 1 minute, scraping up the brown bits on the bottom on the pan.
5. Toss in the tomatoes and cook, stirring occasionally, until they break down, about 5 minutes.
6. Add the tomato sauce and mustard and bring the liquid to a simmer.
7. Stir in the brown sugar and cook for about 3 minutes, until it dissolves.
8. Pour in the root beer, balsamic vinegar, molasses, and vanilla. Bring the liquid to a boil, reduce the heat and simmer for 15 to 20 minutes; you're cooking to bring out the sweetness of the tomatoes.
9. Set aside to cool slightly. Transfer to the jar of a blender and purée until smooth. Return the purée to the saucepan.
10. Stir in the honey, along with the espresso, black pepper, paprika, chili powder, cayenne, allspice, garlic powder, cumin, and the remaining salt. Simmer on low, covered, for 40 minutes to 1 hour, until the sauce is a deep reddish brown. Taste, and add more seasoning as needed. It will keep in the refrigerator in an airtight container for weeks.

Soups + Stews

"I don't know that there is
anything more honest than food"

Tomato Basil Bisque

For all of the food I love, for all the places I've been, and, having to think about recipes that stand out for me as both a chef and a human being for this book, it occurs to me I am really an American and I'm really proud of that. My cooking's American style and with an American flair. Our cooking is very distinctive and, as far as soup goes, to me tomato bisque soup and a grilled cheese is right up there with apple pie; it is as American as you can get and it's just good, simple food and to the point, and exactly what you want. I do eat a lot of soup but this in particular speaks so much to who I am.

MAKES ABOUT 6 CUPS OR
ENOUGH FOR 4 SERVINGS

¼ cup (½ stick) unsalted butter

1 medium or large yellow onion, diced

3 teaspoons kosher salt, plus more to taste

10 to 12 garlic cloves, smashed and roughly chopped

2 pounds heirloom or vine-ripened tomatoes, cooked, and puréed in a food processor or blender

¼ teaspoon black pepper

5 large fresh basil leaves

4 dried bay leaves

1 fresh rosemary sprig

1 fresh thyme sprig

2 fresh oregano sprigs

1½ tablespoons smoked paprika

3 cups low-sodium chicken stock or water

1 cup heavy whipping cream

1. Melt the butter in a large saucepan over medium heat.
2. Add the onions, season with 1 teaspoon of the salt, and cook for about 10 minutes, until tender and translucent, stirring often so the onion doesn't brown.
3. Add the garlic and cook for about 1–2 minutes, stirring constantly, until it is fragrant and golden brown.
4. Stir in the puréed tomatoes and season with the remaining 2 teaspoons salt, pepper, basil, bay leaves, rosemary, thyme, oregano, and paprika. Cook for 5 to 10 minutes, to meld the flavors.
5. Pour in the chicken stock, increase the heat to high, and bring the soup to a boil. Reduce the heat and simmer the soup for 15 to 20 minutes, until the tomatoes are really broken down.
6. Stir in the cream and cook just long enough to warm it, about 3 minutes. Season with more salt to taste. Remove and discard the herbs. Serve warm.

Plátano Soup

Green (unripe) plantains aren't sweet; they don't taste like bananas; the taste of potatoes is the closest I can think of. This soup is rich and hearty and all you will want after eating it is a good, cozy nap.

MAKES 8 TO 10 CUPS OR
ENOUGH FOR 4 TO 6 SERVINGS

2 smoked ham hocks or 1 ham shank, halved (about 2 pounds total)

3 pounds green plantains (7 or 8 plantains), peeled and cut into large segments

2 large yellow onions, diced

8 garlic cloves (about half a head of garlic), smashed

1 tablespoon kosher salt, plus more to taste

3 fresh thyme sprigs

2 long fresh oregano sprigs

¾ teaspoon ground cumin

Freshly ground black pepper

1 cup Ají (see page 45)

1. Put the ham hocks in a large saucepan and add enough water to cover by 2 or 3 inches. Bring the water to a boil over high heat, reduce the heat, and simmer the ham hocks for 1 hour, skimming off the foam that rises to the top.
2. Add the remaining ingredients, except the Ají, and boil until the plantains are tender, about 1 hour 15 minutes.
3. Turn off the heat, remove the ham hocks, and set them aside to cool to room temperature.
4. Purée the soup with an immersion blender and add more salt to taste.
5. Pull the meat off the ham hocks, chop it, and stir it into the soup, with a little left over to decorate each serving. Top with a spoonful or two of Ají and serve warm.

Butternut Squash Soup

I love this soup. Its funny, for the Food Network cooking show we'd bought tons of squash to decorate the set and I thought, "What feels like winter?" Winter vegetables, and of course, tons of pumpkins. Between the prop person and my mom being obsessed with white pumpkin—my mom was here too—we had just gone to the store and we cleaned them out, we got every pumpkin they had. We put them all over the house and put bows on them. When the show was over, I had all this squash, and of course I had to cook it. After a couple weeks of squash this and squash that, my husband and my son were like, "Please, no more!" But there was more. I hate wasting food. We're a member of a vegetable collective that delivers locally grown produce once a week. During the fall and winter months, every single week, there's another butternut squash in our package.

This butternut squash soup was one of the last squash things I made before the season for them was over, and it was such a victory. Even though they were sick of squash, my husband and son both ate it: it was that good. I add cream to the soup but it's also delicious without it.

MAKES ABOUT 4 QUARTS OR ENOUGH FOR 8 SERVINGS

2 butternut squash (about 4 pounds), peeled and cut into 1½-inch cubes (about 7 cups)

1 large Spanish onion, sliced

5 fresh sage sprigs

5 fresh thyme sprigs

3 fresh rosemary sprigs

3 dried bay leaves

1 tablespoon ground ginger

2 cinnamon sticks

4 whole cloves

¼ teaspoon freshly grated nutmeg

2 tablespoons kosher salt, plus more to taste

⅓ cup turbinado (raw) sugar

2 teaspoons curry powder (preferably hot curry powder)

1¼ cups heavy whipping cream (optional)

Thinly sliced almonds, lightly toasted, for garnish

Dried currants or black raisins, for garnish

1. In a large pot, combine the squash, onion, sage, thyme, rosemary, bay leaves, ginger, cinnamon sticks, cloves, nutmeg and salt in a large pot. Add enough water to cover by 1 to 2 inches and bring the water to a boil over high heat.
2. Reduce the heat and simmer for 10 to 15 minutes, until the squash is mushy.
3. Turn off the heat and use an immersion blender to purée the soup.
4. Add the sugar and curry powder and stir until the sugar dissolves.
5. Stir in the heavy cream, if using. Season with more salt to taste. Serve warm, garnished with the almonds and dried currants.

Three-Bean Soup with Ají

Beans are such a staple in Latino cooking; they're something we're known for eating. This hearty, spicy bean soup is something I make all the time using whatever beans I have on hand. It's something I feel good about serving my son because it's so healthy and nourishing. I often make it with beef stock that I make from marrow bones, because my son has eczema and marrow is supposed to be good for eczema. I use a bunch of different types of beans. They take a long time to cook, but the good news is that once you get everything in the pot, you can pretty much leave it alone on the stovetop. It will make the house smell great. The soup is spicy already, but I spoon Ají (page 45) on each serving just to give it that extra kick. I call for you to soak the beans but I often don't plan ahead enough to do this. Un-soaked beans will need to be cooked for a longer time than the time listed in this recipe.

MAKES ABOUT 3 QUARTS OR ENOUGH FOR 6 TO 8 SERVINGS

1½ pounds of assorted dried beans (such as cannellini, black, kidney, pinto, moro, scarlet runner beans), soaked overnight and drained

1 tablespoon Sazón (page 21) or ½ teaspoon achiote paste, crumbled with your fingers

1 tablespoon dried basil

2 tablespoons kosher salt, plus more to taste

1 teaspoon black pepper

¼ teaspoon cayenne pepper

4 dried bay leaves

2 red and 1 green bell pepper, cored, seeded, and diced

1 poblano pepper, cored, seeded, and diced

1 chile verde (aka California green chili), cored, seeded, and diced

3 large tomatoes, diced

2 tablespoons Sofrito (page 75)

3 carrots, trimmed and thinly sliced

Ají (page 45)

1. Put the beans in a large pot with enough water to cover. Bring the water to a boil over high heat, reduce the heat, and simmer the beans until they just begin to soften, about 30 minutes.
2. Stir in the achiote, basil, salt, black pepper, cayenne, and bay leaves, and cook until the beans are very tender, about 1 hour.
3. Add in the red and green bell peppers, the poblano and chile verde, the tomatoes, and sofrito, and cook for about 10 minutes to soften the vegetables.
4. Add the carrots and cook until they just begin to soften, about 5 minutes. Season with more salt to taste and serve this soup on a cold day, with a spoonful of ají topping each bowl.

Ají

Ají is a spicy sauce made of fresh tomatoes and peppers. It's really big in South America. My husband, a Colombian, introduced me to it. It's so easy to make. Just throw everything into a food processor or blender and in no time you have an unbelievably fresh, spicy sauce. I make a big batch and keep it in a Mason jar in the fridge. I like to have it on hand to spoon into soups such as Three Bean Soup with Ají (page 42) and Platano Soup (page 38), or with beans, on Smoked Bacon Arepas, page 22, eggs, tacos.

There's almost nothing it's not good on—except dessert. I can't have tacos without it now. When I went to make it for the first time, my husband and I argued about what was the right way. Then I called his mother and she told me how to do it. I use hers as a base for mine, but of course I had to make it my own. I'm grateful to her, because my husband... well, let's say he was confused. Puerto Ricans eat something called mojo de ajo that I grew up eating. My sister was a foreign exchange student in Argentina and she became obsessed with chimichurri. When my husband first told me about ají, I thought it couldn't be that different than mojo de ajo and chimichurri, but it is. And I'm hooked.

MAKES ABOUT 3½ CUPS

2 habanero peppers, stemmed and roughly chopped (seeds included)

¼ cup distilled white vinegar

Leaves and tender stems of 1 bunch fresh cilantro, roughly chopped (about 2 cups)

½ large Spanish onion, roughly chopped

1 bunch scallions, trimmed and roughly chopped

4 garlic cloves, smashed and roughly chopped

2 tomatoes, roughly chopped

1 tablespoon kosher salt

1 teaspoon black pepper

Juice of 1 lime

1. Put the peppers and vinegar in the bowl of a food processor fitted with a metal blade and pulse to finely chop the peppers. Add the cilantro, onion, scallion, garlic, tomatoes, 2 tablespoons water, the salt, pepper, and lime juice. Pulse to a chunky consistency and serve. It will keep in the refrigerator in an airtight container almost indefinitely.

Coconut Curry Crab Soup

When working on this book, I served this, along with about a dozen other dishes, to a crowd of hungry friends to get their feedback. Everyone loved it! It couldn't be any simpler to make: it's just coconut milk seasoned with lemongrass, curry, and curry leaves, and fresh whole crabs. I don't serve it with rice or anything else; the beauty is in the simplicity. It's so good it's ridiculous.

One of the things about Balinese food is that, if it's crab, there's a whole crab on the plate. Abundance. I love it. It's the entire thing, they might serve it to you with the crab shell being the bowl. It's beautiful. There's something really lush about it that I liked.

INGREDIENT NOTE: Curry leaves, which are integral to Indian cooking, are available at Indian and Middle Eastern food stores. You can find lemongrass, one of the most important flavorings in Thai and Vietnamese cooking, in Asian groceries.

SERVES 4

5 (13.5-ounce) cans coconut milk

2 stalks lemongrass, cut in half lengthwise (see Ingredient Note)

1 curry leaf (see Ingredient Note)

2 tablespoons curry powder

1 tablespoon ground ginger

1 tablespoon kosher salt, plus more to taste

4 whole small crabs

8 ounces lump crabmeat

1. In a very large saucepan over medium heat, combine the coconut milk, lemongrass, curry leaf, curry powder, ground ginger, and salt, and warm until the coconut milk begins to bubble. Reduce the heat and simmer for about 10 minutes to infuse the coconut milk with the flavorings.
2. Add the whole crabs and cook for 15 minutes. Season with more salt to taste.
3. To serve, use tongs to put one crab in each soup bowl. Pour the coconut curry broth over the crabs. Spoon 2 ounces of lump crabmeat on top of each serving. Dig in and enjoy!

Corn Chowder with Lump Crabmeat

Chowder's a classic, but rather than using flour, which is the traditional way of thickening chowder, I add puréed corn and reduce the cream with potato, which releases its starches. This makes for an extra rich and delicious soup that also happens to be gluten free. My mom used to make this for me, and now I make it for my son.

Much like rice is in Asia, corn was the backbone of the Americas for a long time. Living in California, we have access to fresh corn most of the year. Using frozen corn is okay too. I love how versatile it is. There are so many things you can use it for. If given the chance I could write a book all about corn.

MAKES 10 CUPS OR
ENOUGH FOR 4 TO 6 SERVINGS

Kernels cut from 4 ears of corn or 2 cups frozen corn kernels

5 cups vegetable stock

¼ cup (½ stick) unsalted butter

1 medium yellow onion, diced

4 teaspoons kosher salt, plus more to taste

3 garlic cloves, minced

1 large russet potato, scrubbed and diced

1 carrot, diced

6 fresh thyme sprigs

1 cup heavy whipping cream

½ teaspoon black pepper

8 ounces lump jumbo crabmeat

1. In a blender or food processor fitted with a metal blade, purée half of the corn with 1 cup of the vegetable stock. Set aside.
2. Melt the butter in a large saucepan over medium heat. Add the onion, season with 1 teaspoon of the salt, and cook until tender and translucent, stirring often so the onion doesn't brown, about 10 minutes. Add the garlic, season with another teaspoon of the salt, and cook for about 2 minutes, stirring constantly, until it's fragrant and golden brown. Stir in the potato, carrot, thyme, and the remaining 2 teaspoons of salt. Add the remaining 4 cups vegetable stock, the puréed corn, and the reserved corn kernels. Bring the soup to a boil, reduce the heat, and simmer for about 20 minutes, until the soup has thickened slightly and the diced potato is cooked through. Stir in the cream and pepper and cook for about 2 minutes, just to warm the cream. Season with more salt to taste, if necessary.
3. To serve, spoon some crabmeat into the center of each bowl, dividing it evenly. Pour the soup into the bowls at the table.

Chinese Short Rib Soup

My mom used to make an Asian roast pork soup that I loved. This soup, which starts with beef short ribs rather than pork, is a cross between hers and the short rib soup I get in Korea Town in Los Angeles whenever I go to the fabulous Korean spa. (The whole time I'm getting scrubbed down, I'm thinking about what I'm going to eat and drink afterwards: short rib soup and boba, or "bubble tea"—the tea has about 1,800 calories, but the soup makes up for it I'd say!) Cook the soup and noodles separately and serve with the noodles on the side so they don't get soggy and overcooked in the hot broth.

INGREDIENT NOTE: Make sure to buy short ribs on the bone; the bone adds so much flavor to the broth.

SERVES 4 TO 6

2 pounds flanken-cut short ribs (see Ingredient Note), cut into 2–2½-inch segments containing one bone each

1 cup soy sauce

1 large yellow onion, roughly chopped

5 garlic cloves, minced

1 red jalapeño pepper, stemmed and quartered (with seeds)

1 stalk lemongrass (see Ingredient Note, page 46), cut in half lengthwise

2 tablespoons peeled, grated, fresh ginger (use a microplane grater)

¼ cup honey

Handful of scallions, trimmed and thinly sliced on the bias (white and green parts)

Kosher salt, to taste

1 (14-ounce package) vermicelli rice noodles

1. Put the short ribs in a large pot with a lid. Cover the ribs with water and bring to a boil over high heat.
2. Add the soy sauce, onion, garlic, jalapeño, lemongrass, ginger, honey, and scallions. Return the liquid to a boil, reduce the heat, cover the pot, and simmer until the short ribs are fork-tender, about 3 hours. Taste for seasoning and adjust if necessary.
3. Turn off the heat and let the ribs cool slightly in the liquid. Just before serving, cook the noodles according to the package instructions.
4. Serve the ribs and broth warm in shallow bowls, with the noodles on the side.

Lentil & Sausage Stew

I serve these lentils really thick, so they're more like a stew than a soup. If you like heat, the lentils are delicious made with spicy Italian sausage. I go to the butcher's and just ask what they've got—maple smoked, Italian smoked, whatever's fresh, and pork's the most flavorful. I season the sausage meat with cumin, but very little. Cumin has a really wonderful and distinctive flavor, but it can demolish a dish if you use too much. One tip I have for using spices such as cumin (I'd put nutmeg in the same category) is to smell it first. Smelling it will remind you of how pungent it is, and will help prevent you from over-using it.

I've spent a lot of time in Asia, like Kuala Lumpur and Penang, where they do lentils such as dahl, but I wanted to cook them with flavors that I was familiar with, like the rosemary and the sausage, that came to me from living in Italy, going down to Naples. Lentils are not really pricey, but go a long way and we ate a lot of them!

MAKES ABOUT 7 CUPS OR ENOUGH FOR 4 TO 6 SERVINGS

3 tablespoons olive oil

8 ounces Italian sausage, meat removed from casings

1 yellow onion, diced

½ bulb fennel, cored and diced

3 teaspoons kosher salt, plus more to taste

1 pound green lentils

3 cups low-sodium chicken stock

2 large carrots, diced

1 red bell pepper, cored, seeded, and diced

5 garlic cloves, minced

1 teaspoon black pepper

½ teaspoon ground cumin

4 whole cloves

1 stalk celery, diced

1. Heat the oil in a large saucepan over medium-high heat. Crumble in the sausage meat and cook until it's brown all over, breaking it into small pieces with a wooden spoon.
2. Add the onion and fennel, season with 1 teaspoon of the salt, and cook until the vegetables begin to soften and the onions are translucent, about 10 minutes.
3. Add the lentils and chicken stock, and bring the stock to a boil over high heat.
4. Add the carrots, bell pepper, garlic, black pepper, cumin, cloves, and the remaining 2 teaspoons of salt. Cover the pot, reduce the heat to low, and simmer until the lentils are soft, about 30 minutes.
5. Uncover the pot, stir in the celery, and serve.

Beef & Bacon Chili

I make chili often because I make cornbread often (see Skillet Cornbread with Candied Ginger, page 147), and I love a piece of cornbread with chili poured on top. There's a pound of bacon in the chili, and there's nothing wrong with that. The fat rendered from the bacon is used to sauté the onions and other veggies. It's ridiculously rich and delicious. I sometimes make chili with bison instead of beef; trying different meats that I see at the butcher's is fun, just for the sake of trying something new.

MAKES ABOUT 3 QUARTS OR ENOUGH FOR 8 TO 10 SERVINGS

1 pound bacon, chopped

1 large yellow onion, diced

2 pounds ground beef

2 teaspoons smoked salt (or kosher salt plus ½ teaspoon liquid smoke), plus more to taste

1 teaspoon ground black pepper

½ red and ½ green bell pepper, cored, seeded, and diced

2 large vine-ripened tomatoes, diced

1 bunch scallions, trimmed and finely chopped (white and green parts)

3 garlic cloves, minced

2 to 3 tablespoons chili powder, plus more to taste

2 tablespoons smoked paprika

½ teaspoon cayenne pepper

2 dried bay leaves, crumbled

½ cup bourbon

2 (15-ounce) cans dark red kidney beans

1 (28-ounce) can puréed tomatoes

1 quart low-sodium chicken stock or water, or as needed

Shredded cheddar or Gouda cheese for serving

1. Cook the bacon in a large saucepan or Dutch oven over medium heat until the fat is rendered and the bacon is cooked through.
2. Drain the bacon on paper towels.
3. Add the onion and beef to the pot. Season with 1 teaspoon of the smoked salt, and the pepper, and cook, breaking up the meat with a spatula, until it is cooked through, about 10 minutes.
4. Add the bell peppers, season with the remaining 1 teaspoon smoked salt, and sauté for about 10 minutes, until the vegetables are tender, stirring often so they don't brown.
5. Add the tomatoes and scallions and cook for about 5 minutes, until the tomatoes break down.
6. Toss in the garlic and sauté for about 2 minutes, until it is fragrant. Sprinkle the chili powder, smoked paprika, cayenne, and bay leaves into the pan.
7. Stir in the bourbon, beans, and half of the canned tomato purée, and simmer for about 10 minutes.
8. Pour half of the chicken stock into the pot and bring it to a boil over high heat. Reduce the heat and simmer the chili for about 1 hour 30 minutes, adding the remaining tomato sauce and the remaining stock when more liquid is needed, and stirring often.
9. Season with more smoked salt to taste. Chop the bacon and stir it into the chili to rewarm it. Serve in bowls with the shredded cheese sprinkled on top.

Oxtail Stew

This stew is easy to make: you just throw all the ingredients in a pot and cook it for eternity until the meat is falling off the bone. Oxtail stew is easy to turn into oxtail ragù, which can be served over pasta.

I love it and it's funny to me how what used to be considered peasant food. Things like oxtail, for example have recently gotten a new appreciation from restaurants and chefs around the world. I grew up eating oxtail and nothing compares.

SERVES 4

4 pounds oxtail

2 tablespoons kosher salt

1 red and 1 green bell pepper, cored, seeded, and diced

2 yellow onions, diced

6 garlic cloves, smashed

1 tablespoon smoked paprika

½ cup balsamic vinegar

1 tablespoon each of fresh rosemary, thyme, and oregano

1 tablespoon black pepper

1. Put all the ingredients in a large pot or Dutch oven and add enough water to just cover the oxtail.
2. Bring the water to a boil over high heat. Reduce the heat, cover the pot, and simmer the oxtail until the meat is falling off the bones, about 3 hours.
3. Turn off the heat and let the oxtail cool to room temperature in the gravy. Pick the meat off the bones and return to the gravy; discard the bones. Serve warm.

Oxtail Poutine

A twist on my French-Canadian comfort food favorite, my version replaces French fries with yucca fries and smothers them in meat and gravy from the Oxtail Stew recipe below.

SERVES 6

1 large yucca (about 0.6 pounds), peeled and chopped into 1-inch-long strips

Canola or vegetable oil for deep-frying

¼ teaspoon salt for sprinkling, or to taste

4 cups Oxtail Stew (see above)

½ cup grated Manchego

½ cup grated Gruyère

½ cup shredded sharp aged cheddar

1. Bring a medium saucepan of salted water to a boil over medium-high heat, add the yucca, and cook until soft, about 5 minutes. Drain and set aside
2. In another medium pot, heat 2 inches of oil over medium-high heat until the oil reaches 350°F. Prepare a bed of paper towels for draining the fries.
3. Add the yucca strips to the hot oil and flash-fry them until gold and crispy on all sides. Immediately transfer the yucca to the paper towels to drain, and salt them liberally. (Yucca is very starchy, so it's important that this is done right away.)
4. Transfer the hot fries to a platter, spoon the oxtail stew on top (be sure to include both shredded meat and gravy), and sprinkle the grated cheeses all over. Serve immediately.

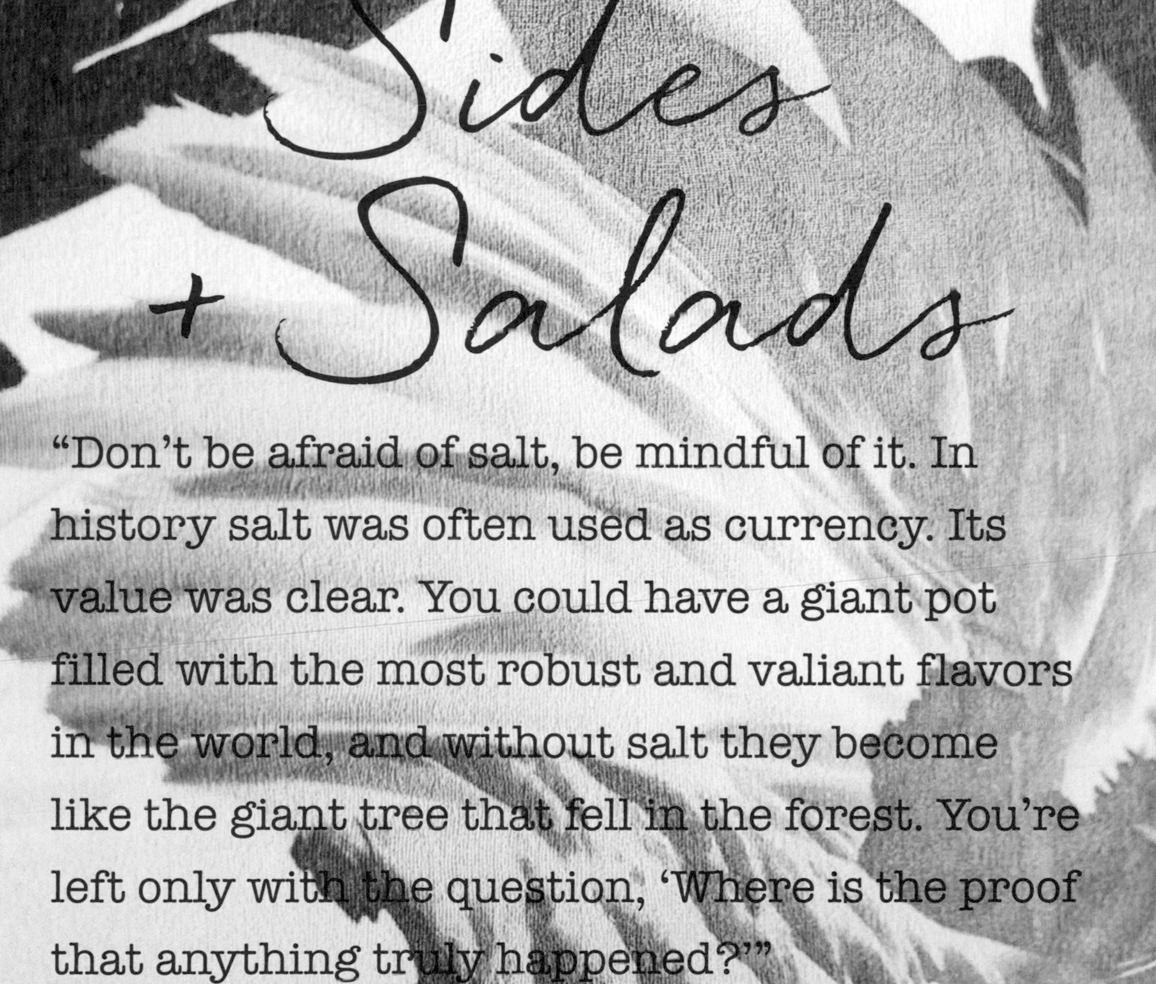

Sides + Salads

"Don't be afraid of salt, be mindful of it. In history salt was often used as currency. Its value was clear. You could have a giant pot filled with the most robust and valiant flavors in the world, and without salt they become like the giant tree that fell in the forest. You're left only with the question, 'Where is the proof that anything truly happened?'"

Matthew 5:13-16

Fried Purple Cabbage

Even though I love them, I didn't grow up eating collard greens, because my mom hates them. Instead, she made many variations of cabbage, which is more Caribbean than greens are. The purple of the cabbage is a gorgeous color—it's like art on a plate—and it looks so pretty with the other Thanksgiving side dishes, which tend to be different shades of brown. I often top the cabbage with a big dollop of mascarpone or goat cheese. The dish looks really pretty that way, and I love the contrasting temperatures of the warm cabbage and the cold, creamy cheese.

SERVES 4 TO 6

½ cup (1 stick) unsalted butter

1 small yellow onion, diced

1 tablespoon sugar

2 teaspoons kosher salt, plus more to taste

½ teaspoon black pepper, plus more to taste

1 head purple cabbage (about 2 pounds), halved, cored, and very thinly sliced

Mascarpone or goat cheese, for garnish (optional)

1. Melt the butter in a large deep skillet or cast-iron pot over medium heat.
2. Add the onion and sprinkle with the sugar along with 1 teaspoon of the salt and ¼ teaspoon of the pepper. Sauté, stirring often, until the onion is tender and translucent, about 10 minutes.
3. Fold in the sliced cabbage and season with the remaining salt and pepper. Increase the heat to high and sauté the cabbage for 10 to 12 minutes, gently tossing it so it cooks evenly, until the cabbage is soft and brown around the edges.
4. Season with more salt and pepper to taste. Top with the mascarpone or goat cheese if you are using it, and serve.

Chorizo Date Stuffing

Even though my mother is my first and biggest influence when it comes to cooking, she is a die-hard traditionalist to the end, whereas I like to deviate. When I started cooking, my mother let me take over the making of Thanksgiving stuffing. That was a long time ago. Now I like to add chorizo, because chorizo and dates is a great match. I start with rustic, whole-grain bread, which gives great flavor and texture to the stuffing. The bread puffs up in the oven like a soufflé, and the top gets crunchy and golden brown. I'm very particular about texture, and don't want to eat something with the texture of wet bread; this is the opposite. A lot of people cut the crusts off bread when making stuffing. I leave it on. I like the different texture it adds to the stuffing.

SERVES 8

4 tablespoons (½ stick) unsalted butter, plus more for greasing the pan

1 pound day-old, whole-grain, rustic-style bread, cut into ¾- to 1-inch cubes

½ cup chopped dried dates (about 6 large Medjool dates)

½ pound hard chorizo, finely diced

½ pound sweet Italian sausage, meat removed from casings

1 medium Spanish onion, finely chopped

1 medium red bell pepper, cored, seeded, and finely chopped

1 medium green bell pepper, cored, seeded, and finely chopped

1 celery stalk, finely chopped

1 large carrot, finely chopped

4 garlic cloves, minced

1 tablespoon plus 1 teaspoon kosher salt

4 cups low-sodium chicken stock

¼ cup fresh Italian parsley or cilantro, finely chopped

1. Position an oven rack in the center and preheat the oven to 350°F. Grease a 3-quart baking dish and set aside.
2. Scatter the bread cubes on two large baking sheets and toast them in the oven until they're dry and golden, about 5 minutes. Set the pans aside to cool the bread to room temperature.
3. Transfer the bread cubes to a large bowl. Add the dates and toss to distribute. Set aside.
4. Meanwhile, melt 2 tablespoons of the butter in a large sauté pan over medium heat. Add the chorizo and Italian sausage and sauté, breaking up the sausage with a wooden spoon or spatula, until the sausage is crumbled and golden brown, about 10 minutes. Add the onion, red and green bell peppers, celery, carrot, and garlic. Season with half of the salt and cook, stirring occasionally, until the vegetables are soft and the onions are translucent, about 10 minutes. Add the remaining 2 tablespoons butter and stir until it melts. Stir in the chicken stock. Add the bread cubes and dates and the remaining salt, and gently stir to coat the bread cubes with the vegetable mixture.
5. Transfer the stuffing to the prepared baking pan and spread it out so the top is even. Sprinkle the parsley or cilantro over the stuffing. Cover the baking dish with foil and bake on the center rack for 30 minutes. Remove the baking dish from the oven, remove the foil, and bake for about 30 minutes more, until the top is golden brown and a toothpick inserted into the stuffing comes out clean. Let the stuffing cool for 10 to 15 minutes before serving.

Eggplant & Asparagus with Five-Spice Plum Sauce

My dad was a vegetarian for most of my lifetime. For my father, my mom used to do a lot of dishes with eggplant because it has a meaty quality that makes vegetable dishes more hearty. I made this dish inspired by those memories, and by the cute baby eggplant that I saw in the market one day. Whenever I see baby eggplant I look for a way to cook them. For this dish, the eggplant and asparagus are stir-fried and then tossed in plum sauce. Serve it with Duck Fried Quinoa (page 101) or plain steamed black rice or Himalayan red rice.

INGREDIENT NOTE: If you can't find baby eggplant, substitute 2 large eggplant, cut in half lengthwise and each half cut into 6 or 8 wedges.

SERVES 6

1 tablespoon toasted sesame oil

8 baby eggplant, quartered (see Ingredient Note)

1 bunch asparagus, stems broken at their natural breaking point, cut into 1½-inch segments

2 teaspoons kosher salt

3 shallots, thinly sliced

1 tablespoon minced garlic

½ cup raw cashews

¾ to 1 cup Five-Spice Plum Sauce (see below)

1. Heat the oil in a large sauté pan over medium heat. Add the eggplant and asparagus, season with 1½ teaspoons of the salt, and cook for 4 to 5 minutes, stirring the pan, until the eggplant begins to brown. Sprinkle the shallots and garlic into the pan, season with the remaining salt, and cook for about 2 minutes, until the shallots are tender and translucent. Add the cashews and enough plum sauce to coat the eggplant, tossing to combine. Serve warm.

Five Spice Plum Sauce

This is my version of hoisin sauce. I toss it into stir-fries and always serve it with Peking Duck (page 103).

MAKES ABOUT 2 CUPS

2½ cups orange juice (preferably with pulp)

1½ cups stewed prunes, pitted, plus ¼ cup of their juice

1 cup sugar

2 tablespoons rice wine vinegar

1 tablespoon Chinese five-spice powder

1 tablespoon minced garlic

1 teaspoon black pepper

1. Combine all of the ingredients in a saucepan and bring to a boil over high heat. Reduce the heat to medium and simmer until the prunes split and the liquid starts to brown, 15 to 20 minutes. (Don't cook so long that the sugar burns.) Set aside to cool slightly. Transfer to the jar of a blender or the bowl of a food processor fitted with a metal blade, and purée until smooth.

Brussels Sprouts with Currants & Almonds

Even though I'm a total carnivore, my body definitely craves green vegetables, and Brussels sprouts are one of my favorites. Probably everybody's mom made a version of Brussels sprouts, but none of them were very exciting back then. Now Brussels sprouts are really trendy and people are making them in all kinds of delicious ways. I cook mine with coconut oil. I also toss in some almonds and dried currants just to keep things interesting, but it's the coconut oil that makes it. The sweet flavor of the coconut oil with the bitter taste of the Brussels sprouts is an unexpected combination, but it's like they were meant to be together. Another thing I like about coconut oil, besides the flavor, is that it's not greasy. I never get tired of them.

SERVES 4

3 tablespoons coconut oil

1 pound Brussels sprouts, prepared and cut in half lengthwise

Sea salt and black pepper

¼ cup finely chopped shallots

1 tablespoon finely chopped garlic

1 tablespoon dried black currants

1 tablespoon slivered almonds

1. Heat a large sauté pan over medium heat for about 1 minute. Add the oil and let it heat up and melt for about 30 seconds until a pinch of salt sizzles when dropped into the pan.
2. Add the Brussels sprouts, cut side down, and season with salt and pepper. Cover the pan and cook the sprouts for about 5 minutes, until the faces are dark brown and caramelized.
3. Remove the lid, scatter the shallots and garlic around the sprouts, season them with salt and pepper, and give the pan a good shake to distribute the ingredients and turn the sprouts. Cook for 1–2 minutes, uncovered, to soften the shallots and garlic, shaking the pan or stirring the vegetables to make sure they don't burn.
4. Stir in the currants and almonds until well combined. Serve warm.

Butternut Squash & Sweet Corn Casserole

I find that when people are looking for a starchy side dish, they automatically go to potatoes or rice, but squash has such great flavor and it's also such a beautiful color, it shouldn't be overlooked. I love butternut squash so much that I could go on and on with all the things you can do with it but here's a good one. The sweet squash and the savory onion in this recipe make for a rich and delicious side dish.

SERVES 6 TO 8

1 (2-pound) butternut squash, peeled, seeds removed and discarded, cut into 1-inch cubes

½ yellow onion, diced

1 ear of corn or ½ cup frozen corn kernels

1 tablespoon kosher salt

½ teaspoon black pepper

½ teaspoon ground cinnamon

1 teaspoon sugar

¼ teaspoon ground cloves

1 teaspoon dried oregano

1 cup heavy whipping cream

¼ cup pecans, lightly toasted and chopped

1 cup shredded Gruyère (about 4 ounces)

1. Position an oven rack in the center and preheat the oven to 350°F.
2. Combine all of the ingredients except the cheese in a large (9- × 13-inch) casserole dish. Cover the dish with aluminum foil and bake the casserole on the center rack for 30 minutes.
3. Remove the dish from the oven, lift off the foil, and sprinkle the top of the casserole with the cheese. Bake the casserole, uncovered, until the squash is fork-tender and the cheese is golden brown and melted, for about 30 minutes longer.

Plantain Mash

Plantains are a fruit in the banana family that are eaten cooked in many different cultures. This plantain side dish makes a really nice, unusual alternative to mashed potatoes; the plantains are boiled until they're soft, drained, and then mashed with butter, cream, garlic, and salt. Reserve the cooking liquid from the plantains and keep in the refrigerator or freezer to use when making rice, thinning a sauce like that in my Jumbo Shrimp with Salsa Criolla and Strawberries (page 133), or in place of water or chicken stock when making soup. The idea of saving cooking water is also something they emphasized in culinary school: they teach you that everything has value and I try to throw away as little as possible.

INGREDIENT NOTE: When shopping for sweet plantains, look for yellowish-black ones. The blacker they are, the better. Green plantains are not as sweet.

SERVES 4

1 teaspoon kosher salt, plus more for the boiling water, and to taste

5 sweet yellowish-black plantains (about 3½ pounds), peeled and cut in half crosswise (see Ingredient Note)

2 cups heavy whipping cream

3 garlic cloves

½ cup (1 stick) unsalted butter, softened at room temperature

½ teaspoon black pepper, plus more to taste

1. Bring a large pot of water to a boil over high heat and salt it to taste like the ocean.
2. Add the plantains, return the water to a boil, and boil until the plantains are very soft when pierced with a fork, 10 to 15 minutes, depending on the ripeness of the plantains.
3. Meanwhile, warm the cream over low heat.
4. Sprinkle the garlic cloves with a big pinch of salt and mince them to a paste. (Salt helps to break down the structure of the garlic, making it easier to mince.)
5. When the plantains are done, drain them, reserving the cooking water for another use, and return the plantains to the pot. Reduce the heat to low, add the butter and garlic paste, and then mash the plantains with a potato masher to break them up. Add 1½ cups of the warmed cream and continue mashing until the mixture is creamy, adding more cream if the mixture seems too dry. Season with more salt, and the pepper to taste, and distribute the seasonings evenly.

Baked Cheese Grits

You may or may not realize that grits and polenta are basically the same thing. Whether you call them grits or polenta, the issue I have with them is that they spread all over the plate when they're served, so you can serve in a bowl or by baking them like this. Baking grits solves that problem. Also, since I add eggs to the grits before baking them, they puff up in the oven so they're almost like a soufflé, which is nice. I usually make these grits as a side dish to go with Shrimp Etouffée (page 135).

SERVES 6 TO 8

3 tablespoons unsalted butter, melted and cooled to room temperature, plus cold butter for greasing the baking dish

1½ teaspoons kosher salt, plus more to taste

1 cup grits (coarsely ground cornmeal)

1 cup whole milk

2 large eggs, lightly beaten

1 cup heavy whipping cream

1½ cups shredded cheddar cheese

1. Position an oven rack in the center and preheat the oven to 350°F. Grease a soufflé dish or deep casserole dish and set aside.
2. In a medium saucepan, bring 3 cups water and the salt to a boil over medium-high heat. Gradually add the grits, whisking constantly, until no clumps remain. Reduce the heat to medium and simmer, stirring frequently, until the grits are thick and creamy, about 5 minutes. Whisk in the milk.
3. Whisk 1 cup of the grits into the beaten eggs and pour the egg and grits mixture back into the pot, stirring constantly. Stir in the cream, melted butter, and cheese until thoroughly incorporated. Season with more salt to taste.
4. Pour the grits into the prepared baking dish and bake on the center rack until the grits are golden brown and puffed up, about 45 minutes. Serve warm.

Carrot & Yam Soufflé

You often hear people say that there's no such thing as American food, but that's just not true. Candied yams, for instances, baked with marshmallows on top, is as American as it gets. I made this side dish, which is a cross between candied yams and carrot soufflé, for a "holiday feast" themed cooking show for television. I ate something similar to this at a little restaurant in Georgia, where I lived for a while, where old grannies go after church and once I discovered it, it's where I went every Sunday after church. The ladies who work there are old and often grumpy. When I would ask them about different things on the menu, they would never give me an answer They would just say, "Little girl, do you want it or not?" I always wanted it, whatever it was. They served a carrot and yam soufflé but they would never tell me how to make it, so I would just order it every week and pick it apart to try to figure out how it was made. This is my version.

Before you do the marshmallows, make a crumble with a stick (½ cup) of butter and 2 to 3 tablespoons (maybe more) of flour, and ½ cup sugar. Add pecans depending on if you like them. When the soufflé is almost done, put this on top, then at the very end add the marshmallows on top. The three different textures: really spectacular.

SERVES 10

¾ cup (1½ sticks) unsalted butter, melted, plus cold butter for greasing the baking dish

3 large yams (about 2 pounds), peeled and coarsely chopped

5 large carrots (about 12 ounces), peeled and coarsely chopped

1 cup heavy whipping cream

1 cup turbinado (raw) sugar

4 extra-large eggs, lightly beaten

½ cup all-purpose flour

1 tablespoon ground cinnamon

2 teaspoons freshly grated nutmeg

1½ teaspoons baking powder

¼ teaspoon kosher salt

1 × 10.5-ounce bag miniature marshmallows

1. Position an oven rack in the center and preheat the oven to 350°F. Grease a 9- × 11-inch baking dish and set it aside.
2. In the bowl of a food processor fitted with a metal blade, finely chop the yams and carrots on high speed. Add the cream, sugar, eggs, flour, cinnamon, nutmeg, baking powder, and salt, and pulse to combine.
3. Pour the batter into the greased baking dish and spread it evenly with a rubber spatula. Bake on the center rack for 15 minutes.
4. Remove the soufflé from the oven and scatter the marshmallows over the top. (If doing the version to the left, scatter the prepared crumble, then top with the marshmallows).
5. Return the soufflé to the oven for another 15 to 20 minutes, until the soufflé has puffed up and the marshmallows are golden brown. Serve warm.

Arroz con Gandules

When I started traveling as a musician, I realized that, whether it's risotto in Italy, fried rice in China, or paella in Spain, every culture has a seasoned, colored rice dish with flavorful ingredients in it. Arroz con gandules, rice with pigeon peas, is "mine." A staple of Puerto Rican cuisine, arroz con gandules is something we as a family identified with. But where some families eat arroz con gandules every day, or at least five days a week, for us it was a special treat because my mom, being a chef, was always cooking up new and different things. It's a simple side dish, but it's very flavorful and it looks beautiful. If you make Pernil: reserve the cooking liquid from the roast and use it in place of water to make this rice.

INGREDIENT NOTE: Gandules, also called pigeon peas, are a legume common in Caribbean cuisine. You can get fresh gandules at Latino grocery stores, particularly where there are large populations of Jamaicans, Puerto Ricans, and Dominicans. If you can't find gandules, use frozen green peas or lima beans instead.

MAKES 8 CUPS OR ENOUGH FOR 8 SERVINGS

¼ cup plus 2 tablespoons extra-virgin olive oil
½ cup Sofrito (page 75)
½ large yellow onion, minced
2½ teaspoons kosher salt, plus more to taste
1 (15-ounce) can pigeon peas, drained and rinsed (you can substitute frozen or canned peas; see Ingredient Note)
2 cups long-grain white rice
3 tablespoons Sazón (page 21) or ¼ teaspoon achiote paste (crumbled with your fingers)
½ teaspoon black pepper, plus more to taste
3 cups low-sodium chicken stock (or reserved juices)

1. Heat the oil in a large cast-iron pot or 6-quart saucepan over medium-high heat. Add the sofrito and onion, sprinkle with ½ teaspoon of the salt, and sauté, stirring often, until the onion is tender and translucent, about 10 minutes.
2. Add the peas and sauté for 2 minutes, stirring often.
3. Add the rice, achiote, pepper, and the remaining 2 teaspoons salt, and cook, stirring often, until the rice is lightly browned, about 3 minutes.
4. Pour in the chicken stock (or a combination of the stock and the reserved juices from a pork roast). Bring the liquid to a boil over high heat, reduce the heat to low, and simmer, covered, until the rice is tender, about 20 minutes.
5. Uncover the pot, add more salt and pepper to taste, and fluff up the rice with a fork.

Sofrito

Sofrito, in Latin cuisine, different than Italian sofrito, is a mixture of garlic, cilantro, onions, and peppers that is all blended up. Sofrito recipes, in my culture, are almost like heirlooms. It's one of the things that every Latin mother has that she wants to pass down to her kids. I have a dear friend who is Dominican, and the conversation that we bonded on was that our moms both used to make sofrito and leave it in our freezers for us. My mom to this day will come over and make a big batch; it's like she's saying, "Now you're okay." Everybody makes sofrito a little differently. This is based on my mother's sofrito but she doesn't have an actual recipe, and I don't remember ever actually learning to make it.

I freeze sofrito in Tupperware, but some people freeze it in ice cube trays and then pop a sofrito cube out of the tray when they need it.

MAKES ABOUT 3 CUPS

2 red bell peppers, cored, seeded, and roughly chopped

1 large Spanish onion, roughly chopped

2 cups fresh cilantro leaves and stems

2 cups fresh Italian parsley leaves and stems

½ cup fresh oregano leaves and stems

15 to 20 garlic cloves (2 ounces or the cloves from 1 head), peeled

3 tablespoons distilled white vinegar

1 teaspoon kosher salt

½ teaspoon ground cumin

1. Purée all of the ingredients in the bowl of a food processor fitted with a metal blade until smooth. (If you use a blender instead, add the herbs halfway into the process of puréeing the ingredients.) Bake in the preheated oven at 275°F for five minutes just to dry out a little. Transfer the sofrito into small airtight containers and refrigerate for up to 1 week, or freeze for up to 3 months.

Truffle Whole-Grain Mac & Cheese

When I was pregnant, I started trying to be more conscious about what I was putting into my body. I'm not a dieting kind of person, but wanted to eat well. I started baking my own bread (What can I say: I had a lot of time on my hands!). And started cooking with and eating things like flax seeds, whole grains, and brown rice. I had also just graduated culinary school. All I wanted to do was stay home and cook things that were delicious and good for me. This mac and cheese, made with whole-wheat penne and four types of flavorful cheese, came out of that period of my life, and now I'm known for my mac and cheese. If I were to ask my husband's friends, my friends, and my family what they want me to make them for dinner or for a birthday, hands down they'd say, "a pan of your mac and cheese." "Okay. I can do that."

COOK'S TIP: It's important to cook the pasta only until al dente for this recipe. The pasta will continue to cook when it bakes in the oven, and the mac and cheese is definitely best when the pasta still has some bite to it.

INGREDIENT NOTE: Truffle salt is a luxurious but handy product consisting of sea salt mixed with black truffle shavings. You can find it at specialty food stores and cheese shops. If you can't locate it, a drizzle of truffle oil is a good substitute.

SERVES 10

½ tablespoon kosher salt, plus more for the pasta water

1 pound whole-wheat penne

2 cups whole milk

1 cup heavy whipping cream

8 ounces sour cream

6 tablespoons unsalted butter, plus more for greasing

½ cup all-purpose flour

3 cups shredded extra-sharp cheddar (about 12 ounces)

1 cup shredded smoked mozzarella (about 4 ounces)

2 cups shredded Gouda and 1 cup shredded Havarti

½ tablespoon truffle salt (see Ingredient Note) or a drizzle of truffle oil

1 jalapeño pepper, stemmed, seeded, and minced

1 sleeve of Ritz crackers (about 3½ ounces)

2 tablespoons unsalted butter, melted

1. Preheat the oven to 375°F. Grease a 9- × 13-inch baking dish and set it aside.
2. Bring a pot of water to a boil and salt it well. Cook the pasta until al dente. Drain and set aside.
3. In a medium saucepan, infuse the milk, cream, and sour cream over medium-low heat until it begins to steam, but don't let it boil. Set aside.
4. Melt the butter in a large saucepan over low heat. Stir in the flour and cook, stirring constantly, for 2 to 3 minutes. Gradually pour in the milk mixture, whisking constantly until no lumps remain. Reserve ¼ cup each of the cheddar and mozzarella. Add all the remaining cheeses to the milk mixture, along with the truffle salt and jalapeño, and stir until the cheeses have melted completely. Add the cooked pasta and toss to combine. Transfer to the prepared baking dish and smooth the top to make it as level as possible.
5. Put the Ritz crackers in a bowl and crush them with your hands. Add the melted butter and stir to combine. Sprinkle the cracker mixture over the casserole, followed by the reserved cheeses.
6. Bake for 35 to 40 minutes, until the top is golden.

Vegetable Buckle

I was performing and doing the New Year's Eve countdown in Kraków, Poland, hilarious and nerve-wracking. An hour before the performance, the producers told me that I had to say "Happy New Year" and do the countdown in Polish. I had no time to practice, and there I was in front of 140,000 people, standing next to the president of Poland. I managed to get the words out. The next day, with my nerves back intact, for the first time I had a savory pancake, which inspired this buckle.

SERVES 8 TO 10

For the vegetables

3 tablespoons olive oil

6 ounces baby potatoes, cut into ¼-inch slices

2½ teaspoons kosher salt

⅛ teaspoon cayenne pepper

1 teaspoon dried thyme

1 carrot, cut into ¼-inch-thick slices

1 large yellow onion, diced and ¼ cup shallots

3 garlic cloves, minced

1 crookneck or zucchini squash, diced

1 pasilla pepper (a medium-hot dried chile pepper), cored, seeded, and diced

½ red and ½ green bell pepper, cored, and diced

1 small head of broccoli, cut into small florets

½ bunch of asparagus, tough ends trimmed, cut into 1-inch segments on the bias

1 cup low-sodium chicken stock

2 cups chopped kale, destemmed

Leaves of 3 fresh thyme sprigs

For the batter

1 cup all-purpose flour

1½ teaspoons chopped fresh rosemary

1 teaspoon baking powder

½ teaspoon each black pepper and kosher salt

1¼ cups whole milk

½ cup (1 stick) unsalted butter

½ cup shredded Gruyère (about 3 ounces)

1. Position an oven rack in the center and preheat the oven to 350°F.

2. To make the vegetables, heat 2 tablespoons of the oil in a large skillet over medium-high heat. Add the potatoes, season with 1 teaspoon of the salt, the cayenne, and thyme, reducing the heat a little if needs be, and sauté until the potatoes start to brown, about 5 minutes. Add the carrot and cook for 5 minutes, until they are softened and the potatoes are cooked through. Remove the potatoes and carrots to a plate and set aside. Drizzle the remaining tablespoon of oil into the pan on medium-high heat. Add the onion, season with ½ teaspoon of the salt, and sauté, until tender and translucent, 5 to 7 minutes. Mince the shallots and sprinkle with the garlic into the pan and sauté for 1 to 2 minutes, until the garlic is fragrant, stirring constantly so it doesn't brown. Stir in the squash, pasilla, bell peppers, broccoli, asparagus, and the remaining salt, and sauté for about 5 minutes to soften the vegetables. Add the chicken stock, kale, and fresh thyme, and bring to a simmer, cooking for about 5 minutes, or until the broth is thick enough to coat the back of a spoon. Turn off the heat. Using a slotted spoon, transfer 2 cups of the sautéed vegetables to a bowl and set aside. Let the vegetables remaining in the pan cool slightly, then purée them with the broth left in the pan using an immersion blender to make a gravy.

3. To make the batter, in a large bowl, mix together the flour, rosemary, baking powder, pepper, and the salt until thoroughly combined. Whisk in the milk.

4. Put the stick of butter in a large (9- × 13-inch or 9-inch round) baking pan. Put the baking pan in the oven to melt the butter, about 3 minutes. Remove the pan from the oven. Pour the batter into the center of pan and let it spread out naturally to cover the bottom of the pan. Spoon the vegetable mixture into different places on the batter so there is some batter visible in between clumps of vegetables. Bake on the center rack for 15 to 20 minutes, until the batter is set and starts to brown. Remove the buckle from the oven and sprinkle the cheese over the top. Bake for 8 to 10 minutes more, until the cheese is melted and crisp in places. Serve with the vegetable gravy.

Fava Bean Pilaf

One of my favorite places to go when I'm on tour is Beirut. I absolutely love it, love it, love it. One of the reasons is the food. Out of all the Mediterranean cuisines, which in general are among my favorites, Lebanese food is just the best. I feel like Lebanese cuisine is the French of the Middle East. It is more refined than other foods of the region. The last time I was in Lebanon, I had a fava and rice dish that I fell in love with. Then I came across the same rice dish at a Middle Eastern restaurant in my neighborhood in Los Angeles. After eating the rice dish a few times, I figured out how to make it at home. It's so simple. I love fava beans, but they have such a short, spring-summer season. Recipes like this one that call for dried fava beans allow me to eat them when fresh aren't in season. You could make this with dried lima beans in place of fava beans.

MAKES 6 CUPS OR ENOUGH FOR 6 TO 8 SERVINGS

2 tablespoons unsalted butter

2 tablespoons olive oil

½ pound dried fava beans, soaked overnight and drained

½ medium yellow onion, minced

2 teaspoons kosher salt

¼ teaspoon black pepper

1 cup long-grain white rice (such as basmati)

2 garlic cloves, minced

3 tablespoons chopped fresh dill

3 cups low-sodium chicken stock

1. Heat the butter and oil in a large skillet over high heat until the butter is melted. Add the fava beans and onion.
2. Season with 1 teaspoon of the salt and ⅛ teaspoon of the pepper and sauté until the onion is tender and translucent, about 5 minutes, stirring often so the onion doesn't brown. Stir in the rice, garlic, and dill, and cook for about 2 minutes, until the rice is translucent.
3. Pour the chicken stock into the skillet and add the remaining 1 teaspoon salt and ⅛ teaspoon pepper. Bring the stock to a boil over high heat. Reduce the heat, cover, and simmer until the rice is cooked, about 15 minutes.
4. Turn off the heat and let the pilaf rest for 5 minutes, covered. Fluff up the pilaf with a fork and serve.

Farro Salad with Ginger Sesame Glaze

I eat a ton of grains. Long before the whole surge in popularity of foods like quinoa and kale, I was using quinoa, as well as others, including farro, bulgur wheat, and barley, to make pizza dough, mac and cheese, and salads, you name it. Farro is similar to barley. It has a chewy texture that I love. I started using it when I was pregnant, but it's now a staple in my house. This salad has a really surprising combination of textures and flavors, including fresh ginger, diced apples, and pancetta. If you want to get a head start preparing this salad, cook the farro and make the vinaigrette the day before you plan to serve.

INGREDIENT NOTE: Acidulated water is water mixed with acid used to prevent oxidation, such as the apples in this recipe, from browning. To make acidulated water, mix 1 teaspoon lemon juice or vinegar with 1 pint of water.

COOK'S TIP: Hot ingredients expand when they're puréed in a blender, so unless you take the right precautions, they will explode in your blender, making a big (and possibly dangerous!) mess. To avoid this, when blending hot liquids, let the mixture you are blending cool for at least 5 minutes before transferring it to a blender. Fill the blender no more than halfway, then put the lid on the blender, leaving one corner open. To be on the extra-safe side, you can cover the lid with a kitchen towel to catch any splatters before turning on the blender.

MAKES 8 CUPS OR ENOUGH FOR 4 TO 6 SERVINGS

3½ cups low-sodium chicken stock

2 cups farro

½ cup (¼-inch cubes) pancetta or bacon (about ½ pound)

1 Granny Smith apple, not peeled, finely chopped, and placed in a bowl of acidulated water (see Ingredient Note)

1 cup frozen green peas, thawed in a colander

1 cup thinly sliced shallots (about 4 medium shallots)

2 garlic cloves, minced

1 pinch of cayenne pepper

Kosher salt and black pepper

1 cup homemade Ginger Sesame Glaze (page 90) or my Bounty & Full Ginger Sesame Glaze (order it online at bounty-full.myshopify.com)

1. In a medium saucepan, bring the chicken stock to a boil over high heat. Add the farro and return the stock to a boil. Reduce the heat, cover the pot, and simmer for 25 to 30 minutes, until the farro is al dente and all the liquid has been absorbed. Transfer the farro to a large bowl and set it aside to cool to room temperature.
2. Cook the pancetta in a sauté pan over medium-high heat until it's crispy. Drain on paper towels and add the pancetta to the bowl with the farro.
3. Drain the apple and add to the bowl with the farro and pancetta. Toss in the peas, shallots, and garlic, sprinkle with the cayenne, and season with salt and pepper. Drizzle with the Ginger Sesame Glaze and toss to combine the ingredients. Serve at room temperature.

Tomato Burrata Salad with Avocado Grapefruit Dressing

I love tomatoes and avocados, and use burrata, which is so creamy and wondrous, any time I can find a way. This isn't a lettuce-based salad. It's more in the Greek or Italian tradition of a salad, where they serve just cucumbers, or in this case, just tomatoes, and call it a salad. The dressing is made of puréed avocados so it's thick and creamy.

SERVES 4

For the vinaigrette dressing

1 avocado, halved, pitted, and peeled

⅔ cup orange juice

⅓ cup extra virgin olive oil

½ cup white balsamic vinegar

1 tablespoon chopped yellow onion

2 teaspoons grapefruit juice

1 teaspoon kosher salt

1 teaspoon black pepper

2 garlic cloves, smashed

1 jalapeño pepper, roughly chopped

1½ tablespoons roughly chopped fresh cilantro

For the salad

3 large heirloom or vine-ripened tomatoes

1 (8-ounce) ball Burrata or fresh mozzarella

Kosher salt and black pepper

¼ cup raw unsalted pistachios

1. To make the vinaigrette, combine all of the ingredients in the jar of a blender and purée until smooth.
2. Cut the tomatoes into quarters and arrange them on a serving platter. Place the cheese in the center of the platter and sprinkle the tomatoes and cheese with salt and pepper. Drizzle about ½ cup of the dressing over the salad, scatter the pistachios over the top, and serve. Leftover vinaigrette can be stored in the refrigerator in an airtight container for several days.

Yellow Beans with Fried Salt Pork

When I'm on tour, sometimes people bring me gifts, some of which make no sense at all, and others that totally make sense. When I was on tour for my album, FOOD, I started getting a lot of food gifts, which was fun. People brought cupcakes, homemade crackers, jams, honeys. In San Francisco, this sweet guy—I think Rob was his name—brought me an entire gift basket of food. He lives in Napa where he told me he has all kinds of friends with all these amazing markets and restaurants. He'd made me a really spectacular gift basket with items from the area: cookies, oils, vinegars, and a lot of really cool dried beans that I'd never seen before. I turned some of the beans into a soup (see Three Bean Soup with Ají, page 45). And I cooked a bag of yellow beans with cubes of fried salt pork and ate the beans as a side dish. They came out so hearty and so delicious. Even though I soaked them overnight, the dried beans took forever to cook. My husband loves to drizzle olive oil on these and every other kind of beans.

MAKES 6 CUPS OR ENOUGH FOR 4 SERVINGS

Canola or vegetable oil for deep-frying

½ cup (½-inch) cubes salt pork

1 pound light-colored dried beans (or any dried bean will work—I like navy beans if I can't find yellow), soaked overnight and drained

½ large Spanish onion, diced

6 garlic cloves, minced

2 large fresh rosemary sprigs

1 fresh thyme sprig

2 teaspoons kosher salt, or to taste

1½ teaspoons black pepper

1 quart low-sodium chicken stock, or as needed

1. Heat the oil in a small saucepan over high heat until it reaches 350°F.
2. Add the salt pork and fry until crisp, 3 to 5 minutes. Using a slotted spoon or strainer, remove the pork from the oil and transfer it to a large saucepan.
3. Add the rest of the ingredients (except the chicken stock) to the saucepan, and enough water to cover the beans by 1 inch. Bring the water to a boil over high heat.
4. Reduce the heat and simmer the beans until they're tender and mushy, adding the stock gradually so the beans are constantly covered with liquid throughout the cooking process, 1 to 1½ hours. Check and adjust the seasoning if necessary.

Kale this and kale that. Kale is everywhere. I don't want to eat something just because it's good for me, it has to taste good too. The crispness of the kale with the sweet graininess of the guava is the perfect match.

INGREDIENT NOTE:
You can often find frozen guava purée sold in bags in grocery stores. If you can't locate it, use mango purée. And if you can't find that, buy frozen cubes of mango and purée them in a blender.

SERVES 4

For the vinaigrette

¼ cup grapeseed oil or extra-virgin olive oil

¼ cup guava purée (see Ingredient Note)

2 tablespoons white wine vinegar or champagne vinegar

2 tablespoons minced shallot (about 1 small shallot)

1 teaspoon Dijon mustard

¼ teaspoon kosher salt

¼ teaspoon black pepper

⅛ teaspoon ground cumin

⅛ teaspoon cayenne pepper

For the salad

1 bunch Tuscan kale (aka black kale), leaves stacked, rolled, and thinly sliced (about 4 loosely packed cups)

½ cup diced heirloom tomato (about half of a medium tomato)

¼ cup diced dried apricots (about 6 medium)

¼ cup coarsely chopped candied pecans (about 14 pecan halves)

¼ small red onion, thinly sliced

1. To make the vinaigrette, whisk together all of the ingredients in a small bowl.
2. In a large bowl, combine the kale, tomato, apricots, pecans, and red onion slices. Drizzle with about 6 tablespoons of the vinaigrette and toss to combine, making sure to coat all of the salad ingredients with the vinaigrette. Add more dressing to taste, if you choose. Leftover vinaigrette can be stored in the refrigerator in an airtight container for several days.

Spinach Salad

with Manchego Cheese & Bloody Mary Vinaigrette

When I did a 31-day raw food cleanse, I got very creative with raw vegetables, salads in particular. I'm such a carnivore that it was definitely a challenge for me to eat as many vegetables as I did that month. In the process, I learned that if the salad contained different textures, especially something chewy and crunchy, it felt more satisfying. I love the texture of raw hazelnuts, so I threw them in a lot of my salads, and also dried fruits. This salad, which contains chopped hazelnuts and dried blueberries, became one of my go-to salads during that period, and one that I continue to make even when I'm not dieting. Of course, now I would add the cheese (wink).

SERVES 4

For the vinaigrette

1¼ cups tequila

1 large (16-ounce) can tomato sauce

⅓ cup sherry vinegar

¼ cup jarred pickled garlic cloves, minced

¼ cup juice from a jar of pepperoncini

¼ cup minced red onion

6 garlic cloves, minced

2½ tablespoons black pepper

2 tablespoons fresh lime juice

2 tablespoons bottled hot sauce (I use siracha or my own Bounty & Full Hot Sauce)

2 tablespoons prepared horseradish

1½ teaspoons smoked salt or kosher salt

For the salad

8 cups pre-washed baby spinach

3 heirloom or vine-ripened tomatoes, chopped

1 yellow bell pepper, halved, seeded, and thinly sliced

1 portobello mushroom, cleaned and very thinly sliced

1 jalapeño pepper, trimmed and sliced into thin rounds

½ cup hazelnuts, chopped

⅓ cup sliced celery

¼ cup dried blueberries

4 ounces Manchego cheese, thinly sliced on a mandolin

1. To make the vinaigrette, bring the tequila to a simmer in a saucepan over high heat and cook for 1 minute to burn off the alcohol. Set aside to cool slightly. Pour the tequila into a medium bowl and whisk in the remaining ingredients.
2. Assemble the salad ingredients except the cheese in a large bowl. Drizzle with ½ cup of the vinaigrette and toss gently to coat and distribute the ingredients. Scatter the cheese slices over the top and serve.

Carrot & New Potato Rösti

After church on Sundays in New York, we used to go to Theresa's, a Polish place on the Lower East Side, for pierogies and blintzes. One of my favorite things were the latkes, or potato pancakes. Later in life, as a result of traveling and going to culinary school, I realized that many cultures make potato pancakes, they just call them by different names. I add carrot to mine; I like the color and sweetness it adds, plus, I'm always trying to sneak vegetables into dishes to get my son to eat them. These make a nice brunch item. Although here I make one large rösti, you can make it in individual pans, which are not only cute, but easier to flip.

SERVES 4

2 large red potatoes (about 1 pound) and 1 large carrot, shredded on the largest hole of a box grater

¼ large yellow onion, minced

4 garlic cloves, minced

2 tablespoons whole-wheat flour

2 teaspoons kosher salt

3 tablespoons ghee or unsalted butter

1. In a large bowl, mix the shredded potatoes and carrots with the onion, garlic, flour, and salt.
2. Melt the ghee in a large sauté pan over medium heat. Tip the rösti mixture into the pan and press gently with a spatula to form the rösti to the shape of the pan. Reduce the heat to medium-low and cook for about 10 minutes, continuing to press on the veggies until the potatoes are deep golden brown and crispy. Flip the rösti and cook the second side, then slide it out of the pan onto a plate, cut it into four wedges, and serve hot.

Ginger Sesame Glaze

I've been making ginger sesame glaze forever. It goes with so many different things. I always have it in my fridge, and now that I have my own sauce line, I always have cases of the Bounty & Full Ginger Sesame Glaze for emergencies. I use it to make Ginger Sesame Glazed Shrimp with Bok Choy (page 134) and Farro Salad with Ginger Sesame Glaze (page 82). It's a great salad dressing.

MAKES ABOUT 1¼ CUPS

¼ cup honey

2 tablespoons toasted sesame oil

2 tablespoons soy sauce

2 tablespoons rice wine vinegar

2 garlic cloves, coarsely chopped

1 large yellow onion, coarsely chopped

1 inch fresh ginger, peeled and coarsely chopped

kosher salt and black pepper, to taste

1. Combine the ingredients in a saucepan and bring to a boil over high heat. Reduce the heat and simmer, stirring, until the garlic and onion are soft. Set aside for 5 minutes to cool. Transfer to the jar of a blender or the bowl of a miniature food processor and blend to a smooth paste. Transfer any leftovers to a glass jar or airtight container and refrigerate for up to 7 days.

Mains

"I didn't really know who I was until I started cooking purposefully. Look at all the people who have traveled to this country to call it home."

Drunken Fried Chicken

This recipe came about when I was researching Peking duck and Korean fried chicken. After learning everything I could about them, I decided to blend ideas and try making a fried chicken of my own creation. It took a lot of failed attempts to get to this, but I did it. The chicken is delicious.

COOK'S TIP: It's important to fry this chicken at a lower-than-normal temperature, otherwise the soy sauce will burn and taste bitter. Use a deep-fry thermometer to ensure the correct temperature.

SERVES 4

2½ cups soy sauce

1 cup rice wine or sake

½ cup honey

½ ounce ginger, peeled and finely sliced

2 tablespoons black pepper

1 tablespoons garlic powder

1 whole chicken, cut into 10 pieces

1 cup potato flour

1 cup rice flour

Vegetable or corn oil for frying (I can't use it because I'm allergic, but peanut oil would be an awesome option too)

1. In a large bowl, whisk together the soy sauce, vinegar, honey, ginger, pepper, and garlic powder. Add the chicken pieces to the bowl and turn to coat them with the marinade. Cover the bowl and refrigerate the chicken overnight or for at least 4 hours.
2. In a large saucepan, heat 3 to 4 inches of the oil until it reaches 350°F.
3. Mix the potato and rice flours together in a large bowl. On the counter, make a bed of paper towels. One by one, remove the chicken pieces from the marinade and put them on the paper towels to drain. Blot off any excess marinade and dredge the chicken in the flour mixture, then fry the chicken in the hot oil, about 8 minutes for smaller pieces, 12 minutes for larger pieces, turning now and then. The chicken will be a deep mahogany color and the juices will run clear when pierced with a small knife. Transfer the chicken pieces to the paper towels to drain.

Orange Chile Chicken

This is my "natural" version of orange chicken from a Chinese restaurant. Serve with brown or white rice.

INGREDIENT NOTE: You can find chile oil in the Asian condiment section of supermarkets. I use chile oil often because it adds a really good, robust flavor to dishes along with its heat.

SERVES 4 TO 6

For the sauce

4 to 5 navel oranges

2 tablespoons canola or vegetable oil

2 tablespoons chile oil (see Ingredient Note)

1½ yellow onions, chopped

2 teaspoons kosher salt, plus more to taste

6 garlic cloves, thinly sliced

3 to 10 spicy chiles (such as red or green serrano or jalapeño peppers, Fresno chiles, Thai red chiles, habanero peppers, or chile pigas), finely chopped, including the seeds

¾ teaspoon smoked paprika

¾ cup sugar

1 quart low-sodium chicken stock, plus more if reheating

¾ cup honey

For the chicken

2 pounds skinless, boneless chicken breast

2 teaspoons kosher salt

2 teaspoons black pepper

1 teaspoon granulated garlic

4 cups all-purpose flour

1 cup cornstarch

3 large eggs, lightly beaten

Canola or vegetable oil for deep-frying

1. To make the sauce, thinly slice 1 orange and set aside. Peel the second orange with a vegetable peeler and thinly slice the zest into julienne. Juice the peeled orange and the remaining oranges into a measuring cup to get ¾ cup juice, and set aside.
2. Heat the canola and chile oil in a large sauté pan over medium-high heat. Add the onion, sprinkle with 1 teaspoon of the salt, and sauté, stirring often, until they are tender and caramelized (golden brown), about 20 minutes. Sprinkle in the garlic and chiles and sauté for about 2 minutes, until the garlic is fragrant, stirring constantly so it doesn't burn. Add the reserved orange slices, orange zest, and the paprika. Stir in the sugar and the remaining salt and cook until the sugar dissolves and begins to bubble, about 2 minutes. Pour in the reserved orange juice and the chicken stock and bring the liquid to a simmer. Stir in the honey, reduce the heat, and simmer until the sauce is the consistency of a glaze (it should be thick enough to coat the chicken), about 25 minutes.
3. While the sauce is cooking, prepare the chicken. In a large saucepan, heat 3 to 4 inches of oil over medium-high heat until it reaches 350°F. Create a bed of paper towels for draining. Cut the chicken into 1½-inch chunks and season with the salt, pepper, and granulated garlic.
4. Pour half the flour into a medium bowl. Whisk the eggs in a second bowl, and combine the remaining flour with the cornstarch in a third bowl. Dredge the chicken pieces in the flour, then the egg, and then in the flour-cornstarch, and put them in a glass baking dish.
5. Working in batches and being careful not to overcrowd the pan, drop the chicken pieces in the oil and fry until golden brown and crisp, about 5 minutes. Transfer the chicken to the paper towels to drain. Cook the remaining chicken pieces in the same way, letting the oil return to 350°F before adding the second batch of chicken.
6. If the glaze is cool, reheat it over medium-low heat, adding more stock to thin it if necessary. Add the chicken pieces to the pan and toss to coat the chicken with the glaze.

Coconut Curry with Chicken & Vegetables

Many years ago, I stayed for a few months at a friend, Rodrigo Otazu's house in Bali, which is where I first encountered this curry dish, but I like to think that over the years, I've made it my own. In this recipe, I call for a whole chicken, cut up. Cooking the chicken on the bone gives the sauce such good flavor. I also think it looks better, seeing meat on the bone rather than little cubes of meat in a sauce. Serve it with white rice or bulgur wheat tossed with golden raisins or black currants. The mix of coconut milk and bulgur makes you feel like you're doing something right for your body. This dish is delicious with lamb or shrimp too.

SERVES 4

1 whole chicken, cut into 10 pieces

2½ teaspoons kosher salt, plus more to taste

1 teaspoon black pepper

1 teaspoon smoked paprika

3 tablespoons coconut oil

1½ large yellow onions, thinly sliced

1 green and 1 red bell pepper, cored, seeded, and thinly sliced

4 cloves garlic, thinly sliced

1 tablespoon grated fresh ginger

¼ cup plus 1 tablespoon packed light or dark brown sugar

3 tablespoons curry powder (preferably hot)

3 carrots, thinly sliced into rounds

8 small fingerling or Yukongold potatoes, halved lengthwise

3 (13.5-ounce) cans coconut milk, warmed over low heat

¼ cup fresh lime juice

1 head of broccoli, cut into florets

Steamed white or brown rice for serving

1 recipe Mango Chutney (page 138)

1. Season the chicken with 2 teaspoons of the salt, ½ teaspoon of the pepper, and ½ teaspoon of the paprika.
2. Heat the oil in a large sauté pan over medium-high heat. Cook the chicken in the hot oil until browned on both sides, about 5 minutes per side. Remove the chicken from the pan and set aside.
3. Add the onions, red and green bell peppers, garlic, and ginger to the pan, season with ½ teaspoon of the salt, and sauté for 3 to 4 minutes, until the vegetables begin to soften. Lower the heat to medium, stir in the sugar, and cook the vegetables with the sugar until they are caramelized, 1 to 2 minutes. Stir in the curry powder.
4. Add the carrots, potatoes, warmed coconut milk, and lime juice and bring the liquid to a simmer. Reduce the heat to low and simmer the curry for 10 minutes to begin to thicken the sauce.
5. Return the chicken pieces to the pan and continue to simmer the curry until it is thick and creamy. Add the broccoli and cook for about 2 minutes, until tender. Taste, and add more salt and pepper to taste. Serve with the steamed rice and chutney.

Malay Curry Chicken

One year, I performed for a Formula One race in Kuala Lumpur. While there, I had some spare time, so I asked one of the chefs at the hotel where I was staying if he would teach me how to make really traditional Malay curry, which is served everywhere from outdoor markets to really fine restaurants and hotels.

SERVES 4

2½ pounds skinless chicken breast, thinly sliced

2½ teaspoons kosher salt, plus more to taste

⅓ cup red curry paste

1 teaspoon ground coriander

½ teaspoon ground cumin

¼ teaspoon ground cardamom

½ teaspoon ground fennel

1 (3-inch) piece fresh ginger, peeled and roughly chopped (about ⅓ cup)

1 cup roughly chopped shallots

8 garlic cloves, roughly chopped

2 tablespoons ghee (or use unsalted butter)

1 tablespoon tomato paste

1 cup low-sodium chicken stock

3 curry leaves (see Ingredient Note, page 46)

2 star anise

1 cinnamon stick

1 cup plain Greek yogurt

1. Slice the chicken breasts into ½-inch-thick pieces and season with 2 teaspoons of the salt. Set aside.
2. In a small bowl, combine the curry paste, coriander, cumin, cardamom, and fennel with enough water to form a thick paste and set aside.
3. In the jar of a blender or the bowl of a mini food processor, combine the ginger, shallots, and garlic, and the remaining ½ teaspoon salt and purée to make a paste. Melt the ghee in large sauté pan over medium heat. Scrape in the contents of the blender or food processor and cook, stirring constantly, until the garlic is fragrant, about 2 minutes. Stir in the spice paste and tomato paste and cook until slightly caramelized, 3 to 5 minutes. Add the chicken stock, curry leaves, star anise, and cinnamon stick, and cook, scraping up the cooked bits from the bottom of the pan, for about 1 minute. Add the chicken, and bring the stock to a boil. Reduce the heat and simmer just to cook the chicken through, about 7 minutes. Turn off the heat. Put the yogurt in a small bowl and gradually add 1 cup of the curry sauce from the pan, whisking constantly. Stir the yogurt mixture back into the curry sauce and chicken, and serve.

Duck Fried Quinoa

My mom is half Chinese, so in addition to Puerto Rican cuisine, I grew up eating a lot of Asian food. Although the quinoa in this dish would really piss her off (she always says, "Quinoa this! Kale that! All these trendy ingredients!"), it was, in a sense, inspired by her, since she taught me to cook with a wok, and to make fried rice. It was also inspired by the meat and bones I had left after making and serving Peking Duck (page 103). If you have leftover duck bones, boil them to make a quick, small batch of duck stock and use that in place of water to make the quinoa.

SERVES 4

2 cups quinoa, rinsed thoroughly

4 large eggs

¼ teaspoon kosher salt

2 tablespoons unsalted butter

3 garlic cloves

4 tablespoons plus 1 teaspoon sesame oil

1 (½-inch) piece fresh ginger, peeled and thinly sliced

¼ large yellow onion, diced

½ carrot, trimmed and diced

4 tablespoons soy sauce

1 to 2 cups shredded duck (you can substitute dark meat chicken)

3 scallions, thinly sliced

½ cup frozen baby peas

¼ cup bean sprouts

1. Bring 2 cups of water to a boil in a small saucepan over high heat. Add the quinoa and return the water to a boil. Reduce the heat to low, cover the pot, and cook until the quinoa is tender and the water is evaporated. Turn off the heat and set aside to rest, covered, for at least 5 minutes.
2. Beat the eggs with the salt. Heat the butter in a large sauté pan (preferably nonstick) over medium heat. Pour in the egg mixture and gently scramble the eggs for 2-3 minutes, taking care not to over-cook them.
3. Mince and set aside 2½ cloves of the garlic, reserving the remaining half. Heat a wok over high heat. Add 1 teaspoon of the sesame oil, along with 1 slice of the ginger and the half garlic clove, using a fork or spatula to drag the ginger and garlic around the wok 4 or 5 times.
4. Add another 1 tablespoon of the sesame oil and let it heat for 1 minute. Sauté the onion in the sesame oil for 5 minutes, until softened, stirring often so it doesn't brown.
5. Toss in the minced garlic and sauté for 1 to 2 minutes, stirring constantly so it doesn't color. Add the carrot and the remaining sliced ginger, and sauté for 2 to 3 minutes to soften.
6. Add 1 tablespoon of the sesame oil and 1 tablespoon of the soy sauce and then gently stir in the duck, quinoa, and scrambled eggs.
7. Add the remaining 2 tablespoons of oil and 3 tablespoons of soy sauce to the wok, along with the scallions, peas, and sprouts, and cook for 1 to 2 minutes to warm the vegetables through.

Crispy Peking Duck

I love duck; it's my favorite of the poultry groups, because it's all dark meat. I've made duck many different ways, but it was fairly recently that I tried making Peking duck for the first time. Peking duck requires a few steps, and that you plan a few days ahead, but it's worth the effort. The key is to dry out the skin, so that when it cooks, the skin gets nice and crispy. To do this, you separate the skin from the flesh. The traditional way is to take a straw, stick it between the skin and flesh, and blow to get air under the skin. I tried but it didn't work for me. I almost gave myself a hernia and the skin didn't separate. Instead, I did it with a wooden spoon.

INGREDIENT NOTE: I use Malta, a malt-based non-alcoholic beverage popular in some Hispanic and South American cultures, to glaze the skin. If you can't find it, use soy sauce instead.

SERVES 4 TO 6

2 tablespoons plus 1½ teaspoons kosher salt

2 teaspoons baking powder

1 whole duck, weighing 4 to 4½ pounds

½ cup Malta (see Ingredient Note) or 2 tablespoons soy sauce

½ cup honey

2 jasmine tea bags

1. Combine 2 tablespoons of the salt and the baking powder in a small bowl. Put a baking rack inside a baking tray.
2. Pat the duck dry with paper towels. Using your hands, carefully separate the duck's skin from the meat, starting at the bottom of the breast and working upward, taking care to keep the skin attached to the duck and also not to tear the skin. Rub the salt and baking soda mixture over the skin of the duck and place the duck on the baking rack set in the baking tray. Refrigerate the duck, uncovered, for 2 to 3 days, until the skin is dry and leathery looking.
3. Position an oven rack as close to the bottom of the oven as possible and remove any racks above it to make room for the duck. Preheat the oven to 350°F.
4. Transfer the duck on its baking rack from the refrigerator to the sink. Fill a pot large enough to hold the duck with water and bring the water to a boil over high heat. Dump half the boiling water over the duck. Turn the duck over and dump the other half of the boiling water on the second side. Set the duck aside on the baking rack with the baking tray underneath to dry for at least 5 minutes.
5. In a small bowl, combine the Malta and honey with the remaining 1½ teaspoons salt and brush the glaze over the surface of the duck. Put the tea bags inside the cavity of the duck. Fill an empty can (such as a beer can) with water and put it in the cavity of the duck so you will be able to set it upright.
6. Set up the baking tray with the baking rack in it as you did before. Break or remove the duck's tail to get the duck to stand up straight. Roast for 1 hour, rotating it from front to back midway through the roasting time so it browns evenly, until it is a deep mahogany color. Reduce the heat to 250°F and continue roasting until fat stops dripping from the cavity, about 30 minutes. Set the duck aside to rest for 10 minutes before carving. If the duck has shrunken around the can, using kitchen shears, cut down the back of the spine so the meat naturally falls from the bone. Don't cut too deep as the can is still inside. Remove it carefully, so as not to spill excess water in the can onto the duck.

Turkey Meatloaf with Ground Walnuts

Meatloaf is totally American. It's hearty. It's simple. And I love it. You can do a million different things in making meatloaf. Beef meatloaf is the most traditional, but in recent years, turkey meatloaf has become a close second. It's so easy to make, and you can serve it for dinner, then have leftover meatloaf in sandwiches the next day. I like to serve this meatloaf with the Whole Grain and Veggie Buckle (page 79) so I can spoon the veggie gravy made from the buckle over the meatloaf.

SERVES 6 TO 8

2 pounds ground turkey

3 medium carrots, trimmed and roughly chopped

½ yellow onion

½ green bell pepper, cored, seeded, and roughly chopped

2 large eggs, lightly whisked

10 ounces walnuts, coarsely ground in a food processor (about 4 cups)

4 garlic cloves, smashed and roughly chopped

1½ tablespoons powdered mustard

1 tablespoon kosher salt

1 tablespoon fresh thyme leaves

3 tablespoons smoked paprika

1 teaspoon black pepper

1. Position one oven rack in the center and preheat the oven to 350°F. Set aside the turkey in a large bowl.
2. In the bowl of a food processor with the metal blade, process the carrots, onion, and bell pepper until very finely chopped. Transfer the vegetables to the bowl with the turkey. Add the eggs and half of the ground walnuts along with the garlic, mustard, salt, thyme, paprika, and pepper, and mix with your hands until thoroughly incorporated. Shape the meatloaf mixture into a football-shaped loaf with your hands. Coat the meatloaf with the remaining walnuts and put the loaf on a baking sheet.
3. Bake the meatloaf on the middle rack for about 1 hour, or until the center of the meatloaf registers 160°F on an instant-read thermometer. Let cool slightly before slicing and serving.

Herb-Larded Turkey

Larding sounds intense but it's really injecting or just adding fat and flavor to the meat. It gives the turkey a beautiful color and the larding helps keep the turkey moist and flavorful, especially the juices left in the pan. The turkey's delicious in sandwiches with Mandarin Orange Cranberry Sauce.

I celebrate Thanksgiving in the sense that I cook. I like that it is an American day for family and people to get together and just share a moment. For me, especially being in California—and I'm not from here, I have a lot of friends who live here who are not from here—I usually take in all the people who don't have family around either, and it feels like home. It's a day to eat and get together.

Ingredient note: Achiote or Annatto (*Bixa orellana*) is a Brazilian tree and the seeds are used in cooking, bringing a nice golden color to the turkey here; the flavor is bitter and you just want to use a small amount of seeds, ground to a powder.

SERVES 8 TO 10

1 (12- to 14-pound) turkey

1 bunch fresh rosemary, leaves finely chopped, plus extra for the cavity

1 bunch fresh thyme, leaves finely chopped, plus extra for the cavity

¾ cup Sazón (see page 21) or achiote paste, crumbled with your fingers

1 tablespoon smoked paprika

8 garlic cloves, smashed

1 tablespoon coarse ground pepper

2 tablespoons kosher salt

½ cup olive oil

¾ cup (1½ sticks) unsalted butter, softened

2 yellow onions, quartered

2 green bell peppers, halved and seeded

1 recipe Mandarin Orange Cranberry Sauce (page 138)

1. Adjust the oven rack to the lowest position and remove other racks if necessary. Preheat the oven to 325°F.
2. Remove the turkey parts from the breast and neck cavities and pat the bird dry with paper towels. Set the turkey aside to come to room temperature.
3. In a small bowl, combine the herbs, achiote paste, paprika, garlic, pepper, salt, oil and butter, mashing the seasonings with the butter and oil to create a rub. Work the rub under the skin of the turkey and massage it into the breasts, legs, and cavity. Massage the rub on the outside of the skin as well. Stuff the turkey cavity the with quartered onions, bell peppers, and extra herbs. With kitchen twine, tie the legs together over the back of breast and tuck in the ends of the wings so they will be protected during cooking.
4. Roast the turkey for 1 hour. Reduce the heat to 300°F and roast for another 1 hour 40 minutes, or until a thermometer inserted into the thickest part of the thigh registers 165°F. Remove the turkey from the oven, transfer to a large platter, cover loosely with foil, and let rest 30 minutes before carving. Serve with the cranberry sauce on the side.

Jerk Ribs with Brown Sugar Rub

When I moved to LA, I really found myself craving Jamaican food. In Harlem, it's readily available, but here, sadly, there just wasn't a good Jamaican restaurant. Even when friends suggested them, I'd go and try, and think, "This is not good…actually this is bad." I like food from warm climate places; like the people, the flavors are bold and loud, full of spice. They use a lot of flavors, colors, spices and I just have an affinity to them. One day, I was especially craving Jamaican jerk, a seasoning blend that includes allspice, garlic, thyme, and other spices—every version's a bit different. I'd given up on finding decent Jamaican food in LA, so I experimented to make my own. Jerk is normally used with chicken but, since I'm a huge rib lover, I tried the same idea with ribs! I first rubbed them with a spicy brown sugar mix and then coated them in sauce made with soy sauce, toasted sesame oil, garlic, thyme, molasses, and allspice. I brought the ribs to the studio one day when I was recording my last album. The whole band went wild over them. It's all we could talk about all afternoon, so I named the song we were working on that day "Jerk Ribs." It was the first single released off that album. The ribs are great. The song is pretty awesome too.

The Brown Sugar Rub is just delicious; you can put it on bacon, steak, lamb chops, meats. It's bold flavors.

INGREDIENT NOTE: You might be surprised that I ask you to add the entire thyme sprigs, stems and all, to the blender when making the sauce. The stems are actually where the most flavor is in the herb and where the most oils are, and when they're all blended up, they give the sauce its body.

SERVES 4

For the ribs

2 racks pork ribs (preferably St. Louis-style ribs; 2 to 3 pounds each)

1 tablespoon kosher salt

1 teaspoon smoked paprika

½ cup Brown Sugar Rub (see opposite)

For the sauce

½ cup toasted sesame oil

¼ cup molasses

2 tablespoons soy sauce

2 teaspoons ground allspice

4 to 6 garlic cloves, peeled

1 to 2 Scotch bonnet or habanero peppers, seeded or whole (using the seeds will make the sauce very spicy)

1 bunch scallions, trimmed and coarsely chopped

1 bunch fresh thyme sprigs (see Ingredient Note)

½ teaspoon black pepper

1. Position 2 oven racks in the center and preheat the oven to 400°F.
2. Season both sides of the ribs with the salt. Stir the smoked paprika into the spicy rub and coat both sides of the ribs with the rub. Place the ribs, bone side down, in a large baking dish. Cover the dish tightly with aluminum foil and roast the ribs on the center rack for 2 to 2½ hours, rotating the baking dish from the top to the bottom racks halfway through so they cook evenly. The ribs are done when the meat separates easily from the bone.
3. While the ribs roast, make the jerk sauce. Combine all of the ingredients in the jar of a blender or the bowl of a food processor fitted with a metal blade and purée until smooth. Transfer the jerk mixture to a saucepan and bring it to a boil over high heat. Reduce the heat

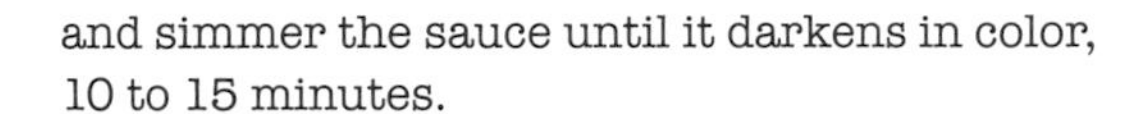

and simmer the sauce until it darkens in color, 10 to 15 minutes.

4. Remove the ribs from the oven, but do not turn it off. Remove the foil but don't discard it. Using a basting brush or the back of a spoon, coat the ribs evenly with the jerk sauce. Cover the dish with the aluminum foil again and roast the ribs for 15 minutes more. Serve the ribs with the rest of the sauce on the side.

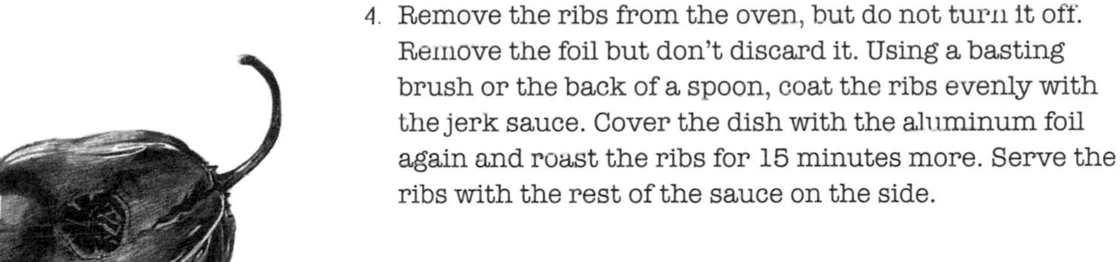

Brown Sugar Rub

This rub is delicious--it has just enough caraway to offset the sweetness. I make it in big batches, so I always have some on hand, and use it to rub on stewed chicken, lamb chops, or steak. It just makes everything taste great. If you sprinkle it on bacon before cooking, it will change your life. The rub is light on salt because I like to salt meat directly and then add the rub, and this way I don't accidentally over-salt. Caraway, like cumin or nutmeg, is one of those seasonings that you have to be very sparing with. A little tastes amazing, but go too far and it'll overpower whatever you're making. When I'm cooking with these spices, I start by smelling the spice to remind myself how strong it is every time. Our sense of smell is a great measuring tool. Balance is key.

MAKES 1½ CUPS

1 cup light or dark brown sugar

2 tablespoons whole caraway seeds

2 tablespoons granulated garlic

2 tablespoons kosher salt

2 teaspoons cayenne pepper

1. Mix all of the ingredients together in a medium bowl. Use immediately or store in an airtight container at room temperature for up to several months.

Pernil: Puerto Rican Pork Shoulder

Pernil is my favorite thing in the world. My grandmother made it. My mom made it. And now I make it. Make sure you get a pork shoulder with the skin on and bone in. When you slice into the roast, you see the gorgeous olives and garlic in every slice. I call for a 6- to 8-pound roast, but make any size pernil you want; I like to have leftovers for sandwiches. Make a special order from your grocery store or butcher. It's hard to find large roasts sometimes, so order from your butcher ahead of time. My butcher orders it for me every other month and texts me when it comes in. Reserve the juices to make Arroz con Gandules (Page 72).

SERVES 10 TO 12

For the rub

¾ cup (1½ sticks) unsalted butter, softened

¾ cup achiote paste or Sazón (page 21)

½ cup olive oil

2 tablespoons kosher salt

1 tablespoon coarse freshly ground black pepper

1 tablespoon minced fresh rosemary

1 tablespoon minced fresh thyme

1 tablespoon smoked paprika

1 tablespoon onion powder

1 tablespoon dried oregano

1 tablespoon ground cumin

For the pork

1 (6- to 8-pound) bone-in, skin-on pork shoulder

¾ cup whole small pimento-stuffed olives

6 garlic cloves, smashed

2 cups low-sodium chicken stock or water, or as needed

1. To make the rub, combine the butter with the rest of the ingredients and mash into the butter to make a paste.
2. To prepare the pork, rinse the pork shoulder under cold running water and pat it dry with paper towels. With a large sharp knife, stab the pork all over the surface, including the top, bottom, and sides, penetrating about 2 inches into the flesh. Using your hands, rub the paste all over the pork shoulder, working the mixture into the slits and under the skin. Lard the pork with the olives and garlic in the slits. Place the pork, skin side up, in a large roasting pan, cover with plastic wrap, and let marinate in the refrigerator for a minimum of 3 hours or up to 2 days.
3. When you're ready to roast the pork shoulder, adjust an oven rack to the lowest position, removing other racks if needed. Preheat the oven to 400°F.
4. Remove the pork from the refrigerator and let it sit for 30 minutes to bring it to room temperature. Pour enough chicken stock or water into the pan to come about 1 inch up the sides of the pork. Cover the pan tightly with aluminum foil and braise the pork for 3 hours, or until the meat is tender. Take the pork from the oven. Remove and discard the foil, and return it to the oven to roast, uncovered, for 1 hour, or until the skin is dark brown and crisp. Set the pork aside to rest for at least 10 minutes before serving. Reserve the juices to make Arroz con Gandules (page 72). Slice the pork and serve.

Chicharrón

Chicharrón refers to fried pork belly; it's very common in Latino cooking. Slice it and eat it as a main dish with rice or mango, monchengo, beans or polenta, or use it to make sandwiches. Ask your butcher for a whole pork belly with the skin on. Slice it and spoon Ají (page 45) on it. It's fatty, meaty, and wonderful.

SERVES 4 AS A MAIN DISH

1 whole skin-on pork belly (1½ to 2 pounds)

3 tablespoons kosher salt

1 tablespoon black pepper

2 tablespoons garlic powder

2 tablespoons onion powder

Canola or vegetable oil for deep-frying

1. Pour 3 quarts of water into a baking dish large enough to hold the pork in a single layer. Stir in the salt, pepper, garlic powder, and onion powder. Put the pork belly in the brine, cover, and refrigerate for 3 days, turning the pork daily.
2. Remove the pork belly from the brine and pat it with paper towels to dry. Make a bed of paper towels for draining.
3. In a large saucepan, heat 4 inches of oil over medium heat until it reaches 350°F. Gently slide the pork belly into the oil and fry for 20 to 30 minutes, until the skin is hard and crackling to the touch. Remove the pork from the oil and set it, skin side up, on the paper towels to drain the oil and cool it slightly. Slice the chicharrón and use it to make a sandwich, serve it with beans, or cut it into cubes and snack on it.

Tostones

Known as Patacones in Colombian cuisine, I grew up on these and my husband also loves them. Common in all Latin American countries. It's like a perfect marriage. Chicharrón and tostones.

SERVES 4

Olive oil for deep frying

4 plantains, peeled

1 lemon, juiced

Kosher salt

1. Heat the oil over a high heat in a medium size skillet. Cut the plantains in half lengthwise and lay them into the oil and fry for around 3-4 minutes—they need just to be colored, and not cooked through.
2. Remove the plantains and pat dry on paper towels to remove excess oil.
3. Place them on a board and smash each half plantain with another board or with a tostonera if you have one. Then lay them on a clean towel and evenly coat them with freshly squeezed lemon juice.
4. Reheat the oil, add the plantains, and re-fry until cooked all the way through—around 4 to 5 minutes. Take out with a slotted spoon, and salt immediately. They should be golden colored and crispy.

Burrata-Stuffed Meatballs with Pistachio Basil Pesto

I was a judge on Top Chef Masters one year, and one of my favorite dishes was a stuffed meatball. I borrowed that idea for these meatballs, which are stuffed with burrata (cream-filled mozzarella), and tossed with a beautiful, bright green pistachio pesto. I use a combination of beef, veal, and pork. It's the traditional Italian way. I use leftover meatballs and pesto to make sandwiches.

COOK'S TIP: I have a little miniature food processor that I use exclusively for mincing garlic when I need more than just one or two cloves, such as for this recipe.

MAKES ABOUT 2 DOZEN MEATBALLS OR ENOUGH FOR 6-8 SERVINGS

1 pound ground pork

1 pound ground beef

1 pound ground veal

½ red onion, minced

6 garlic cloves, minced

1 tablespoon dried oregano

1 tablespoon plus 2 teaspoons kosher salt

1 tablespoon smoked paprika

2 teaspoons dried basil

1 teaspoon black pepper

1 cup fresh breadcrumbs

8 ounces Burrata

2 tablespoons olive oil

1 recipe Pistachio Basil Pesto (page 139), at room temperature

1. In a large bowl, mix together the pork, beef, veal, red onion, garlic, oregano, salt, smoked paprika, basil, and pepper, massaging the mixture with your hands to incorporate the ingredients without smashing the meat too much. Put the breadcrumbs on a plate. To shape the meatballs, take 2½ ounces of the meat and gently form a patty. Scoop a scant teaspoon of burrata into the center, fold up the edges, and gently roll the meat into a ball. Roll the balls in the breadcrumbs and put them on a baking sheet. For perfectly round meatballs, put the meatballs in the refrigerator for at least 1 hour and up to overnight to chill; chilling helps them hold their shape when cooked.

2. Heat the oil over medium heat in a large sauté pan with a lid. Gently tap the excess breadcrumbs from the meatballs, put the meatballs in the oil, and brown them on all sides, 6 to 8 minutes. Cover the pan, turn off the heat, and let the meatballs cook all the way through from the residual heat in the pan, about 8 minutes. Remove the lid, pour the pesto over the meatballs, and turn them gently to coat with the pesto. Serve immediately.

Swedish Meatballs

I've worked in Sweden a lot. I love Stockholm, and I love Swedish meatballs. I can't normally eat the same thing every day, but since meatballs are just about the only Swedish food I like, I eat these, mashed potatoes, and lingonberries every day. The meatballs have a slight sweetness to them, and great texture, and anything with a brown, creamy gravy is great. Most people I know have only had Swedish meatballs from IKEA. They're not bad, actually, for a frozen product, but they're nothing compared with the real thing. Naturally, I had to learn to make my own.

MAKES ABOUT 4 DOZEN MEATBALLS OR ENOUGH FOR 6 TO 8 SERVINGS

For the meatballs

2 slices wheat or white bread

½ cup whole milk

5 tablespoons unsalted butter

½ large yellow onion, minced

2½ teaspoons kosher salt

1 pound ground pork

1 pound ground beef

1 teaspoon ground nutmeg

1 teaspoon ground allspice

2 large eggs, lightly beaten

For the gravy

½ cup (1 stick) unsalted butter

2 tablespoons all-purpose flour

2 cups beef stock

1⅓ cups heavy cream

1. Preheat the oven to 200°F.
2. To make the meatballs, cut the crust off the bread and tear the bread into small pieces into a bowl. Pour the milk over the bread and set aside.
3. Melt 1 tablespoon of the butter in a medium sauté pan over medium heat. Add the onion, season with ½ teaspoon of the salt, and sauté, stirring often, until the onion is soft and lightly browned, about 12 minutes. Add the onion to the bowl with the bread.
4. In a large bowl, mix together the ground meats, remaining 2 teaspoons salt, and the nutmeg and allspice, incorporating the seasonings into the meats with your hands. Add the bread mixture and the eggs to the bowl and massage the ingredients together with your hands to combine.
5. Form the meat mixture into bite-size balls (about 1-ounce each) and place them on a baking sheet. For perfectly round meatballs, put the meatballs in the refrigerator for at least 1 hour and up to overnight to chill to help the meatballs hold their shape when cooked.
6. Warm 2 tablespoons of the remaining butter in a large sauté pan over medium-high heat until it bubbles but doesn't brown. Add half of the meatballs and pan-fry them until they are brown all over and cooked through, about 10 minutes. As they are done, transfer the meatballs to a baking sheet or heatproof plate and keep warm in the oven. Heat the remaining 2 tablespoons butter and cook the remaining meatballs in the same way, transferring to the oven with the first batch.
7. To make the gravy, wipe out the pan you cooked the meatballs in. Melt the butter over medium-low heat. Stir in the flour and cook, stirring with a whisk, until the flour is lightly browned, about 2 minutes. Gradually pour in the beef stock, stirring constantly with the whisk, and cook until the gravy begins to thicken, about 10 minutes. Pour in the cream and cook until the gravy is thick enough to coat the back of a spoon, about 2 minutes. Remove the meatballs from the oven and add them to the pan with the gravy. Turn to coat the meatballs on all sides with the gravy, and serve.

Oxtail & Wild Mushroom Ragù

Italian food is so much more than tomato sauce, pasta, pizza, that kind of thing. But what Italian food is really, changes depending on where you are. When I was in Naples, I had a lot of stewed oxtails. They were very different from the oxtails I ate growing up (see Oxtail Stew, page 35), but they were delicious, and they were the inspiration for this ragù. In the North, Italians eat more polenta than you might think.

MAKES 4 CUPS OR ENOUGH FOR 6 SERVINGS

1 recipe Fresh Spinach Pasta (page 125)

Semolina flour for dusting

1 tablespoon unsalted butter

¼ yellow onion, cut into small dice

1 celery stalk, cut into small dice

1 carrot, cut into small dice

1 teaspoon kosher salt, plus more to taste

¼ teaspoon black pepper

1½ cups thinly sliced wild mushrooms (such as beechwood, chanterelle, shiitake, porcini, or cremini; about 1½ pounds)

1 cup shredded oxtail meat and ½ cup gravy, reserved from Oxtail Stew (page 55)

1 cup Arrabiata Sauce (page 124)

Wedge of Parmesan for grating

1. Roll out the pasta dough and cut it into fettuccini. Transfer the pasta to a baking sheet and sprinkle with semolina flour to prevent the strands from clumping together. Cover and refrigerate the pasta until you're ready to cook it, or for up to 3 days.
2. Melt the butter in a large skillet over medium heat. Add the onion, celery, and carrot, sprinkle lightly with the salt and pepper, and sauté for about 5 minutes, until the vegetables have softened. Add the mushrooms and cook for about 10 minutes, until they darken slightly and look heavy with the pan juices. Stir in the oxtail meat and gravy, along with the arrabiata sauce, and cook and stir to distribute the meat and warm the sauce through, 3 to 5 minutes. Season with more salt to taste. Set aside while you cook the pasta.
3. Bring a large pot of water to a boil and add enough salt so it tastes like the ocean. Drop the pasta in the boiling water, stir so it doesn't stick together, and cook for 45 seconds. Drain the pasta and add it to the skillet with the ragù. Toss to coat the pasta with the sauce. Transfer the pasta to serving plates and grate Parmesan over the top. Serve immediately.

Pineapple Beef

When I was about 15 years old, I worked near a restaurant on the Upper West Side in Manhattan called Penang. My two favorite dishes there were shrimp with mango and beef with pineapple. It was my first encounter with Malaysian food, and it would be a long time before I realized that Penang was a place. Malaysia was a far-off land to me. I couldn't fathom what it would be like to be there. Fast forward just two years, I signed my first deal, and before I knew it, I was in Penang. I couldn't believe I was actually there! I loved the food at Penang the restaurant and in Penang the city, but it also became a symbol for me of how far I'd come. Before I ever had a career, before I knew what I was going to do with my life, I used to go to this restaurant for lunch and eat pineapple beef, and now here I was sitting on a beach in this really exotic, beautiful country. I felt in awe of life and how things turn out. This dish and that trip has stayed with me all of these years. Since then I've been able to travel to that part of the world extensively and there are so many luscious treasures to taste.

SERVES 4 TO 6

3 rib-eye steaks, frozen, and sliced ¼ inch thick

2½ teaspoons kosher salt

3 teaspoons black pepper

2 tablespoons unsalted butter or ghee

1 tablespoon chile oil

½ large yellow onion, coarsely chopped

1 pineapple, peeled, cored, and cut into 1-inch chunks

1 green bell pepper, cored, seeded, and coarsely chopped

1 tablespoon finely grated fresh ginger

3 garlic cloves, minced

1½ teaspoons ground cumin

1 teaspoon curry powder

½ cup pineapple juice

3 tablespoons soy sauce

2 tablespoons turbinado (raw) sugar

2 cups sugar snap peas or snow peas, strings removed

4 spring onions or scallions, thinly sliced on the bias (white and green parts)

¼ cup chopped fresh cilantro

Steamed white or brown rice for serving

1. Season the steaks with 2 teaspoons of the salt and 1 teaspoon of the pepper and set aside.
2. Melt the butter with the chile oil in a large sauté pan over medium-high heat. Add the onion, season with the remaining ½ teaspoon salt, and sauté, stirring often, until it begins to soften, about 5 minutes. Toss in the pineapple, bell pepper, ginger, garlic, cumin, and curry powder, and cook for about 5 minutes, until the bell peppers soften. Stir in the pineapple juice, soy sauce, and sugar. Bring to a simmer and cook for about 2 minutes to thicken the sauce. Increase the heat to high, add the steak, and cook for about 1 minute. Stir in the peas and scallions, and cook for about 2 minutes to warm them through and take off the raw edge. Turn off the heat and stir in the cilantro. Serve with white or brown rice.

Pastelón with Sweet Corn Béchamel

Pastelón, which is a layered casserole of platanos and picadillo (ground meat mixture), is a traditional casserole in Puerto Rican and Dominican cooking and you won't find it in a restaurant. It's something that you'll have at someone's house—their mother made it; you can never tell her that it isn't right—her grandmother gave her the recipe. There's no right and wrong here! I use a combination of green plantains, which taste a bit like potatoes, and yellow, ripe plantains, obviously sweet. I serve it with Sweet Corn Béchamel because I think everything needs sauce and it plays to the sweetness of the ripe plantains and the saltiness of the olives. Pastelón is a bit tedious to make, but you make a big casserole dish of it and it'll last you for a few days. I add chorizo to the meat mixture; I got the idea after my mom told me about a dish of plantains stuffed with chorizo. The contrast between the sweet plantains and the spicy chorizo is amazing. The best way to describe Pastelon is like a Puerto Rican lasagna or cusende – for lack of a better description. It's not something you've tried in festivals, it's something your mother would make and everyone makes it different. Here's how I do it.

SERVES 6 TO 8

6 to 8 plantains, half of them yellow, half green

Kosher salt for the boiling water

Canola or vegetable oil for deep-frying

2 tablespoons olive oil

½ large Spanish onion, minced

¾ teaspoon black pepper

1 chile verde (California green chili), seeds and membrane removed, minced

1 pound ground beef

1 pound soft chorizo sausage, meat removed from casings

1 tablespoon saffron threads

2 teaspoons Sazón (page 21) or ¼ teaspoon achiote paste, crumbled with your fingers

1 teaspoon finely chopped fresh oregano

½ teaspoon ground cumin

4 ounces hard chorizo, diced

3 tablespoons roughly chopped, green, pimento-stuffed olives

Butter for greasing the baking dish

6 large eggs, separated

1½ cups heavy whipping cream

5 ounces shredded extra-sharp cheddar

1 recipe Sweet Corn Béchamel (page 123)

1. Score the peels of the yellow and green plantains lengthwise and remove and discard the peels. Slice ⅛- to ¼-inch thick lengthwise, keeping the yellow and green separate.
2. Lay the green plantain slices flat in the bottom of a large pot and fill it with water. Make a bed of paper towels for draining. Bring the water to a boil over

high heat, salt it to taste like the ocean, and boil the plantains until tender, about 30 minutes. Drain them and put them on paper towels to dry.

3. In a large, straight-sided sauté pan, heat 2 inches of oil over medium-high heat until it reaches 350°F. On the counter, make a bed of paper towels. Slide the yellow plantains into the oil and fry until they are golden brown but still soft inside, 8 to 10 minutes. Transfer to paper towels to drain.
4. Heat the olive oil in large skillet (preferably cast iron) over medium heat. Add the onion, season with ¼ teaspoon of the pepper, and cook, stirring often, until tender and translucent, about 10 minutes. Add the chile verde, beef, chorizo, saffron, achiote, oregano, and cumin, and cook until the meat is cooked through, breaking up the meat with a wooden spoon, about 5 minutes. Stir in the hard chorizo and olives. Turn off the heat and strain the fat from the meat, spooning out the grease with a large spoon. Set aside while you prepare the other components of the casserole.
5. Grease the bottom and sides of a large baking dish with butter. Lay the plantain slices in the dish in a single layer as you would noodles for lasagna, alternating between green and yellow. Spread 1 cup of the meat mixture over the plantains. Lay down another layer of the plantains and another layer of meat until you have built three layers and used all of the plantains and meat.
6. Whisk the egg yolks, cream, and remaining ½ teaspoon pepper together in a small bowl or glass measuring cup and pour evenly over the casserole. Scatter the cheese over the top. Bake the pastelón for 20 to 25 minutes, until the cheese bubbles and browns and the egg is set. Set the pastelón aside to cool for 5 to 10 minutes before serving. Serve hot, cut into squares, with the béchamel on the side.

Sweet Corn Béchamel

Béchamel is one of the mother sauces in French cooking. I learned these in culinary school but who says we have to stick to the rules? When I make béchamel to serve with pastelónes, I add corn; I like the textural component and the burst of sweet flavor.

MAKES 4 CUPS

¼ cup (½ stick) unsalted butter

½ cup minced shallots (about 3 medium shallots)

1 teaspoon kosher salt, plus more to taste

¼ cup all-purpose flour

3 cups whole milk

1 cup fresh or frozen corn kernels

1. Melt the butter in a medium saucepan over low heat but be sure it doesn't brown. Cook the shallots with the salt, stirring often so the shallots don't brown, until they are tender and translucent, 4 to 5 minutes.
2. Stir in the flour, whisking until no lumps remain. Cook, stirring constantly, until the flour is very light golden, about 3 minutes.
3. Gradually add 1 cup of the milk, whisking until incorporated. Pour in the remaining milk and a good pinch of salt, and bring the milk to a boil. Reduce the heat and simmer, stirring with a rubber spatula so the sauce doesn't scorch on the bottom of the pan, until it is thick enough to coat the back of the spatula.
4. Stir in the corn and cook for about 2 minutes to warm it through. Add more salt to taste.

Fresh Spinach Pasta with Arrabiata Sauce

The process of making pasta to me feels like a love thing. It's not a quick fix. You start in the morning and you take a day to make it. Once I make the dough, I'll keep a boule of it in my freezer. I feel like if you're going to go to the process of making things such as pasta dough from scratch, it's a treat to have some leftover in the freezer.

MAKES ABOUT 3 POUNDS

6 ounces fresh spinach

1½ cups semolina flour

1 cup all-purpose flour

2 large eggs

½ teaspoon kosher salt

1. Steam the spinach and set aside to cool to room temperature. Squeeze the spinach in your fists to extract as much water as possible. Put the spinach in the bowl of a food processor fitted with a metal blade and chop to a paste.
2. Combine the semolina and all-purpose flours on a flat work surface. Make a crater in the center of the flour and crack the eggs into the crater. Add the spinach and salt and work them in with a fork until no flour is visible. Add 1 tablespoon water and knead the dough, gradually adding an additional 2 tablespoons water, or more as needed (you want it to be moist like Play-Doh but not wet or sticky), until the dough feels elastic, about 10 minutes. Form the dough into a ball and wrap it tightly with plastic wrap. Chill the dough in the refrigerator for about an hour. Roll it out on a lightly floured surface, then pass it through a pasta machine and cut or form the pasta dough to whatever shape your heart desires. The thinner the pasta, the shorter the cook time.

Arrabiata Sauce

Arrabiata means "angry" in Italian and refers to a simple, spicy tomato sauce flecked with red pepper flakes for heat. I lived in Rome for a while, so I've tried all the traditional Italian sauces. But since I'm not Italian, I don't feel the need to stick to tradition. Back in Los Angeles, when I decided to make an arrabiata sauce, I figured: I live in California, so I might as well use what's available to me. For my arrabiata, I made this spicy, chunky tomato sauce using habanero peppers and chile oil for heat instead of chili flakes. I toss the sauce with pasta (you can use any dried pasta shape) on its own, and also use it along with shredded oxtail to make a spicy, meaty ragù.

MAKES ABOUT 4 CUPS

1 tablespoon chile oil

1 tablespoon olive oil

2½ pounds Spanish onion (about 4 large onions), diced

2 tablespoons kosher salt, plus more to taste

½ red bell pepper, cored, seeded, and diced

2 habanero peppers

2 garlic cloves, minced

½ cup red wine

3 pounds heirloom or vine-ripened red tomatoes, diced

1 cup canned or jarred tomato sauce

2 fresh rosemary sprigs

⅓ cup fresh basil leaves

2 tablespoons dried oregano

2 tablespoons black pepper

1 teaspoon smoked paprika

1 recipe Fresh Spinach Pasta (see opposite)

1. Heat the chile oil and olive oil in a large sauté pan over medium heat. Sauté the onions, seasoning them with some of the salt, and stirring often, until tender and dark golden brown, about 15 minutes. Add the bell pepper, habanero peppers, and garlic, season them with some of the remaining salt, and sauté, stirring often, until the peppers are soft, about 3 minutes. Pour in the wine and cook for 1 minute, stirring up any brown bits on the bottom of the pan. Add the tomatoes and the remaining salt, and cook until they soften and break down, about 5 minutes. Stir in the tomato sauce, rosemary, basil, oregano, black pepper, ½ cup water, and paprika, reduce the heat to low, and simmer for about 15 minutes to meld the flavors.
2. To cook the pasta, take half the recipe opposite and sheet into linguine or spaghetti on a pasta machine. Boil a large pot of well-salted water, drop in the pasta, and cook for 6 minutes or until just al dente. Drain, and serve in bowls with sauce on the top.

Crab & Ricotta Ravioli with Roasted Bell Pepper Sauce

I worked on the line in a restaurant in Los Angeles for a short period of time, and one of my jobs was to make the crab mousse ravioli. I didn't actually like the mousse, but I got really good at making ravioli—because I made hundreds of them. You can serve these as a main course, or, if you're doing an Italian themed night, serve just two or three on a plate as an appetizer. You can also flash fry them, which is a really special treat.

SERVES 4 AS A MAIN DISH; 8 AS AN APPETIZER

1 tablespoon unsalted butter

2 large shallots, minced

2 teaspoons kosher salt, plus more for the pasta water

8 ounces lump crabmeat

8 ounces fresh ricotta

¼ teaspoon red chili flakes

Spinach Pasta Dough (page 125)

Semolina flour for dusting

2 large egg yolks

1 recipe Roasted Bell Pepper Sauce (page 128)

Wedge of Parmesan for grating

1. Melt the butter with the shallots in a medium sauté pan over medium heat. Sprinkle the shallots with 1 teaspoon of the salt and sauté until they are soft and caramelized, about 10 minutes, stirring often so they don't crisp. Set the shallots aside to cool to room temperature.
2. Combine the crab, ricotta, chili flakes, shallots, and the remaining salt in a large bowl and gently fold the ingredients together using a rubber spatula to ensure a light and fluffy filling.
3. Roll out the spinach pasta dough into ⅛-inch-thick sheets. Stack the sheets on a baking sheet, sprinkling with semolina flour between each sheet to keep them from sticking together.
4. Whisk the egg yolks with 2 tablespoons of water to make an egg wash.
5. You can make ravioli in whatever size or shape you want using a ravioli or cookie cutter. For 2-inch square ravioli, lay a sheet of pasta on your work surface. Brush a light layer of egg wash over the surface of the dough. Spoon 2 teaspoons of the filling in mounds along the center of the dough, leaving 1½ inches between each mound. Put a second piece of dough on top. Use a ravioli cutter to cut between the mounds to make individual ravioli. Pinch the edges of the dough together to seal, transfer to a baking sheet, and dust with semolina flour until you're ready to boil the ravioli. Continue making ravioli until you've used all of the filling. Leftover dough will keep, wrapped in plastic in the refrigerator, for several days, or you can freeze it.
6. To cook the ravioli, bring a large pot of water to a boil and salt it to taste like the ocean. Drop the ravioli into the water and cook for 1 to 2 minutes, until the pasta is tender. Lift the ravioli out with a slotted spoon or strainer and transfer them to paper towels to drain.
7. To serve, spoon ¼ or ½ cup of the sauce on each plate (amount varies depending on if you're serving the ravioli as an appetizer or a main dish). Lay the ravioli over the sauce, dribble with a little extra virgin olive oil, and grate Parmesan on top.

Roasted Bell Pepper Sauce

I made this sauce as something that would be my answer to traditional Italian tomato-vodka sauce. Instead of tomatoes, it's made with roasted red peppers, which I love. The resulting sauce is rich, delicious, flavorful, and colorful. And one thing—it's not acidic like tomato sauce is. I serve it with Crab Ravioli (page 127) but it also makes an amazing sauce to serve alongside chicken.

MAKES ABOUT 3½ CUPS

3 red bell peppers

3 tablespoons unsalted butter

1 red onion, chopped

1 teaspoon kosher salt, plus more to taste

4 garlic cloves, minced

1 tablespoon black pepper

1 teaspoon Sofrito (page 75)

1 cup low-sodium chicken stock

1 cup heavy whipping cream

½ teaspoon dried oregano

½ cup grated Parmesan cheese

1. Put the bell peppers directly on the burner of a gas stove over high heat until they are charred on all sides and collapsed, turning with tongs to cook evenly, 8 to 10 minutes. (Alternatively, roast the peppers on a grill or in a 400°F oven until they have charred all over and collapsed.) Set the charred peppers aside in a bowl, covered tightly with plastic wrap, to steam for 10 to 15 minutes. (Steaming makes them easier to peel.) Peel the peppers and remove and discard the cores and seeds.
2. Melt the butter in a large sauté pan over medium-low heat. Add the red onion, season with ½ teaspoon of the salt, and sauté, stirring often, until tender and translucent, about 10 minutes. Add the garlic, pepper, sofrito, and roasted peppers, season with the remaining ½ teaspoon of salt, and sauté for 2 minutes, until the garlic is fragrant, stirring constantly so the garlic doesn't brown. Stir in the chicken stock, cream, and oregano. Bring the liquid to a simmer over medium heat, reduce the heat, and simmer for 10 minutes to thicken the liquid. Set aside to cool for at least 5 minutes. Transfer the contents of the sauté pan to the jar of a blender and purée until smooth. Sprinkle in the cheese and pulse to combine. Season with more salt to taste.

Fried Lobster Tails with Garlic Aïoli Tartar Sauce

The first time I ever had deep-fried lobster tails was at a really nice restaurant in Georgia. I'm more of a crustacean person than a fish person myself, so when I saw fried lobster tails on the menu, it seemed like the obvious choice. It's so decadent and indulgent, it almost seems rude. When you serve it to friends, they're always excited by the idea. Fried. Lobster. Now that's luxury. You will need four wooden skewers for deep-frying the lobster tails.

SERVES 4

Canola or vegetable oil for deep-frying—lots!
1½ cups all-purpose flour
2 teaspoons kosher salt
½ teaspoon black pepper
½ cup cornmeal
1 teaspoon kosher salt
4 lobster tails
2 large eggs, lightly beaten
1 recipe Garlic Aïoli-Tartar Sauce (see below)

1. Fill a large saucepan with oil and heat the oil over medium-high heat until it reaches 350°F. On the counter, create a bed of paper towels.
2. Meanwhile, pour 1 cup of the flour into a medium bowl. Add the salt and pepper and stir to combine. Whisk the eggs in a second bowl. Mix the remaining ½ cup flour with the cornmeal in a third bowl.
3. Remove the top and bottom shells of the lobster tails but leave the ends of the tails intact. Dredge each tail in the seasoned flour, then dip it in the beaten egg, then into the flour-cornmeal mixture. Run a skewer through the lobster tails and cut the skewers so they don't stick out more than 1 inch on each side of the tail.
4. Carefully drop each lobster tail into the oil and fry for about 5 minutes, until golden brown and crisp. Transfer the tails to the paper towels to drain and keep warm. Remove and discard the skewers and serve hot, with the aïoli on the side for dipping.

Garlic Aïoli-Tartar Sauce

Being a saucier, I've made aïoli a million ways. So many different combos can bring something simple to life.

MAKES ABOUT 2 CUPS

4 large egg yolks
1½ cups olive oil
2 tablespoons fresh lemon juice
1 teaspoon minced garlic
½ teaspoon kosher salt, plus more to taste
½ teaspoon black pepper
¼ teaspoon red chili flakes
½ cup finely chopped sour dill pickles
½ stalk celery, finely chopped

1. Put the egg yolks in a glass or stainless steel mixing bowl that fits over a medium saucepan. Fill the saucepan halfway with water and bring the water to a boil over high heat. Remove the pan from the heat and place the bowl with the egg yolks on the pan. (If there is so much water in the pan that the bottom of the bowl touches the water, pour out some of the water.) Whisk the egg yolks to break them up.
2. Add one third of the oil slowly, whisking constantly to form an emulsion. Add a few drops of the lemon juice and continue whisking. Whisk in the remaining oil. Add the remaining lemon juice, garlic, salt, pepper, and chili flakes, and whisk to combine. Stir in the pickles and celery. Season with more salt to taste.

Jumbo Shrimp in Salsa Criolla with Strawberries

Salsa criolla is one of my favorite sauces. I used to do it with chicken, but when traveling more, I noticed that a lot of cultures make salsa criolla with fish. When I lived in Spain we would eat whole fish in a rich, red salsa criolla; it was beautiful. There are so many different versions of it depending on where you are in the world. I started adding strawberries one summer when having a Labor Day barbecue for friends and was making the sauce in a massive pot; there, on the counter, were strawberries and I thought, "What a beautiful, robust summer dish. The red strawberries with the yellow peppers, the green rosemary." With all those colors, it's really a gorgeous dish. To me, this is what food should look like.

SERVES 4

2 tablespoons canola oil
¾ teaspoon chili oil
½ large Spanish onion, thinly sliced
1½ teaspoons kosher salt, plus more to taste
½ bunch small carrots, peeled and thinly sliced lengthwise
4 garlic cloves, sliced
½ green, ½ red, and ½ yellow bell peppers, cored, seeded, and thinly sliced
2 large vine-ripened tomatoes, chopped
½ teaspoon ground cumin
½ teaspoon hot smoked paprika
½ teaspoon sweet smoked paprika
2 fresh rosemary sprigs
¼ teaspoon black pepper, plus more to taste
2 tablespoons Sofrito (page 75)
2 pounds jumbo shrimp in their shells, deveined
½ teaspoon achiote paste, crumbled
1 cup vegetable stock or water (or cooking water from Mashed Plantains, page 68)
1 cup large strawberries, hulled and halved

1. In a large saucepan, heat 1 tablespoon of the canola oil with half of the chili oil over medium-high heat. Add the onion, season with ½ teaspoon of the salt, and cook, stirring, until it begins to soften, about 5 minutes. Add the carrots and cook until they begin to soften, about 5 minutes, then add the garlic and green, red, and yellow bell peppers, and cook until soft, about 5 minutes. Stir in the tomatoes, then sprinkle in the cumin, both paprikas, and rosemary. Reduce the heat to low and simmer until all the vegetables are soft and fragrant, about 10 minutes. Season with the rest of the salt, and the pepper, and set aside.

2. Meanwhile, heat the remaining chili oil in another large sauté pan. Add the sofrito, and cook until heated through, about 1 minute. Add the shrimp, sprinkle with the achiote, and stir to mix thoroughly. Pour in the stock and simmer until the shrimp turn pink and opaque, about 5 minutes, adding the strawberries halfway through. Then put the sautéed vegetables back into the pan with the shrimp, stir gently to combine, and serve.

Ginger Sesame Glazed Shrimp with Bok Choy

I started making this shrimp dish as a really quick and delicious meal, using my Bounty & Full Ginger Glaze. It obviously takes a bit longer if you make the sauce from scratch, but it's totally worth the time. It's an Asian dish that looks really beautiful, as though it has a load of little jewels in it.

SERVES 4

3 tablespoons toasted sesame oil

1 green bell pepper, cored, seeded, and thinly sliced

4 large garlic cloves, thinly sliced

1¼ teaspoons kosher salt, plus more to taste

10 ounces large shrimp (16–20 count), peeled and deveined

½ cup homemade Ginger Sesame Glaze (page 90)

2 heads bok choy, ends trimmed and discarded, quartered

¼ cup pomegranate seeds (optional; you can substitute dried cherries or dried cranberries)

1. Heat 1 tablespoon of the sesame oil in a large sauté pan over medium heat. Add the bell pepper and garlic, season with ¼ teaspoon of the salt, and cook for about 3 minutes, until the pepper softens, stirring often so the garlic doesn't brown.
2. Increase the heat to medium-high, add the remaining 2 tablespoons of the sesame oil, and the shrimp, season with the remaining salt, and cook until the shrimp is pink and cooked throughout, about 5 minutes.
3. Pour in the sesame glaze and toss to coat the shrimp well.
4. Add the bok choy and cook for 2 to 3 minutes, until it wilts. Season with more salt to taste.
5. Serve the shrimp with the pomegranate seeds sprinkled on top.

Shrimp Étouffée

I was reacquainted with shrimp étouffée not long ago, when doing a show in New Orleans. I forgot how delicious it was and, after eating it there, came home and made it for my family. It's so good, and it's easy to make. Make shrimp stock from shrimp shells if you start with fresh shrimp in the shell. But I'm a big believer in "do what you can." If you don't have the time to make stock, use vegetable stock or store-bought fish stock instead. Get the freshest shrimp you can.

SERVES 4

For the stock

1½ pounds large shrimp

1 large onion, cut into chunks

1 stalk celery, cut into chunks

1 carrot, cut into chunks

For the étouffée

½ cup (1 stick) unsalted butter

½ cup all-purpose flour

2 large yellow onions, diced

4 teaspoons kosher salt, plus more to taste

3 vine-ripened or heirloom tomatoes

1 red bell pepper, cored, seeded, and diced

1 yellow bell pepper, cored, seeded, and diced

2 stalks celery, diced

1½ tablespoons chopped garlic (from about 6 cloves)

3 dried bay leaves

2 teaspoons chopped fresh oregano

1 teaspoon fresh thyme

½ teaspoon cayenne pepper

1. To make the stock, peel and devein the shrimp, reserving the shrimp shells and tails. Cover the shrimp and refrigerate.
2. Put the shrimp shells and tails in a large saucepan or stockpot. Add the onion, celery, and carrot, and enough water to cover by several inches. Bring the water to a boil over high heat, reduce the heat, and simmer, skimming off the impurities that rise to the top, for 1 hour. Strain and discard the contents of the colander.
3. To make the étouffée, melt the butter with the flour in a large Dutch oven or another large heavy-bottomed pot over medium heat and cook, stirring constantly so the flour doesn't burn, until the flour is the color of caramel, about 10 minutes.
4. Add the onions with 1 teaspoon of the salt and cook for about 5 minutes, stirring often, to soften. Add the tomatoes, red and yellow peppers, celery, garlic, bay leaves, oregano, thyme, cayenne, and 1 teaspoon of the remaining salt and cook for 2 to 3 minutes to break down the tomatoes.
5. Stir in the stock and the remaining 2 teaspoons of salt and bring to a boil over high heat. Reduce the heat and simmer for about 45 minutes, until the liquid begins to thicken.
6. Add the shrimp and cook for 5 to 7 minutes, until they are cooked through. Season with more salt to taste. Serve hot.

Knight-Style Tuna Melt

This recipe is great and also works well with chicken or turkey. My son Knight loves to cook with me in the kitchen, and he's my favorite helper. He loves tuna melts so we make this together. I love it too. It's a nice spin on a modern classic.

MAKES 4 CUPS OR ENOUGH FOR 8 SANDWICHES

For the tuna salad

3 (4-ounce) cans white tuna packed in water, drained

¼ cup golden raisins

¼ red onion, cut into small dice

1 stalk celery, cut into small dice

¼ tart green apple, cut into small dice

1 tablespoon minced garlic

¼ cup raw, unsalted pistachios, roughly chopped

¼ cup plus 2 tablespoons mayonnaise

1½ tablespoons curry powder

1½ teaspoons kosher salt, plus more to taste

¼ teaspoon cayenne pepper

For the sandwiches

4 sandwich-size ciabatta rolls, split in half, or 8 slices rustic white or whole-wheat bread

¼ cup (½ stick) unsalted butter, softened at room temperature

4 slices Swiss or Havarti cheese

1. To make the tuna salad, combine all the tuna salad ingredients in a large bowl and mix thoroughly.
2. If you're using ciabatta, butter the outer sides of the bread. If you're using sliced bread, butter one side of each slice with butter. Put the ciabatta halves or 8 slices of the bread, buttered side-down, on your work surface and spoon ½ cup of the tuna salad on each. Lay 1 slice of cheese on each sandwich.
3. Heat a large skillet over medium heat. Working in batches that will fit in the skillet, grill the sandwiches until they are golden and the cheese is melted. Serve hot.

Mango Chutney

I learned a lot about chutney when I was in Kuala Lumpur some years ago. Until then, I didn't know that chutney is a broad term that refers to many types of condiments, and that what we think of as chutney is what is known in the East as "English chutney." Mango is a classic. I love it.

MAKES ABOUT 2 CUPS

1 teaspoon ghee (or unsalted butter)

½ yellow onion, chopped

½ teaspoon kosher salt

1 large mango, peeled, pitted, and diced

¾ cup turbinado (raw) sugar

1 tablespoon curry powder

2 teaspoons grated fresh ginger

½ teaspoon ground coriander

½ teaspoon ground cumin

1½ tablespoons apple cider vinegar

1. Heat the ghee in a medium saucepan over medium heat for about 1 minute.
2. Add the onion, season with the salt, and sauté, stirring constantly, until the onion begins to soften, about 5 minutes. Add the mango and cook for about 2 minutes.
3. Stir in the sugar, curry, ginger, coriander, and cumin, and cook, stirring, until the sugar melts and begins to bubble. Reduce the heat to medium-low and cook for 3 to 5 minutes, stirring often, until the sauce thickens. Stir through the vinegar and season with more salt to taste. It will keep, refrigerated in an airtight container, for a few months.

Mandarin Orange Cranberry Sauce

I'm proud to say that I have never eaten canned cranberry sauce, ever. Canned cranberry sauce has never made sense to me because it is so easy to make, no reason not to. Cook the cranberries with vanilla to give it a nice round flavor, and add mandarin orange segments because I love the flavor with cranberries, and the colors look so beautiful together. The other thing about cranberry sauce is: why do we only see it at Thanksgiving? It's so tasty, and so versatile. I use it as a glaze for shrimp on the grill, or for roast chicken. I spoon it into vinaigrettes if I want a touch of sweetness, and baked goods, such as Olive Oil Cranberry Cakes with Candied Orange Slices (page 151). This sauce is great in turkey, ham, or roast beef sandwiches. I often serve it on a cheese board; it goes with just about any cheese. I pretty much always have some of this sauce in my refrigerator.

MAKES ABOUT 2 CUPS

Grated zest of 4 mandarin oranges or 1 large orange, plus 1 cup fresh squeezed mandarin or orange juice

1½ cups sugar

¼ teaspoon kosher salt

2 (12-ounce) bags fresh or frozen cranberries

1 tablespoon pure vanilla extract

1. Combine the mandarin juice, sugar, ½ cup water, and salt in a medium saucepan and bring the liquid to a boil over high heat. Stir in the cranberries, mandarin zest, and vanilla. Reduce the heat to low and simmer for 20 to 30 minutes, stirring occasionally, until the cranberries have broken down and the juices have thickened to a sauce consistency. Serve the sauce warm or at room temperature. It will keep, refrigerated in an airtight container, for several weeks.

Whiskey Pear Glaze

This is a delicious sweet and savory glaze for a smoked, clove-studded ham. Equally you can rub it on lamb or roast beef for a dinner party or I use it with pork chops and apple sauce to kick it up a notch.

MAKES ABOUT 2 CUPS

3 pears, peeled, seeded, and chopped

1 tablespoon yellow onion, roughly chopped

1 garlic clove, smashed and roughly chopped

1 teaspoon sea salt

⅓ cup sugar

1¼ cups whiskey

small sprig fresh rosemary

3 whole cloves

1 cinnamon stick

½ teaspoon black pepper

1. Fill a large saucepan with 1 inch of water and bring to a boil over high heat.
2. Cook the pears, onion, garlic, and salt in the boiling water for a couple minutes. Sprinkle the sugar into the pan, stir to combine, and cook, stirring occasionally, until the sauce begins to thicken. Stir in the whiskey.
3. Add the rosemary, cloves, cinnamon stick, and pepper and cook until the pears are soft and mushy, about 5 minutes. Discard the rosemary, cloves and cinnamon stick, and set aside for 5 minutes to cool.
4. Purée in the jar of a blender or the bowl of a food processor fitted with a metal blade until smooth.

Pistachio Basil Pesto

Although they're great, sometimes pine nuts are overpowering, but I love pistachios. It's not traditional, but pistachio texture is crunchy and adds to the green. it looks beautiful, tastes amazing with a nutty added flavor. I came back from Turkey and Israel and they use pistachios so much in desserts. I thought: what else can I do with them? That's how I started using pistachios instead of pine nuts. Turns out the pairing of pistachios and basil is fantastic.

MAKES ABOUT 2 CUPS

6 ounces fresh basil (about 8 packed cups)

1 cup raw unsalted pistachios

2¼ cups extra-virgin olive oil

6 to 8 garlic cloves, smashed and roughly chopped

2 ounces spinach (about 2 packed cups)

½ cup finely grated Parmesan cheese (about 2 ounces)

1 teaspoon kosher salt, plus more to taste

1. Combine all of the ingredients in the bowl of a food processor fitted with a metal blade, or the jar of a blender, and purée. Season with more salt to taste.

Sweet treats

"I never knew the love that
these could bring me"

Cappuccino Cheesecake

with Gingersnap Crust & Dulce de Leche Topping

I do a lot of cheesecakes, but this is by far the most popular. I smear dulce de leche over the top and decorate the edges with chocolate chips. It's so rich and delicious. I prefer to use vanilla beans to vanilla extract. After scraping out the beans, I put the pod in a bowl of sugar to make vanilla sugar. Or—a trick from the older ladies in the Dominican Republic—I put the scraped pods in a pot of water and simmer for the best air freshener ever. Latinos make dulce de leche by simmering a can of sweetened condensed milk for 3 hours. Nothing works better, and it couldn't be easier.

SERVES 8 TO 10

For the crust

5 tablespoons unsalted butter, melted, plus more cold butter for greasing the pan

2 cups chocolate or gingersnap cookie crumbs (about 9 ounces cookies)

½–¾ cup sugar, depending on desired sweetness

For the cheesecake

2 packages (8 ounces each) cream cheese, softened at room temperature

16 ounces mascarpone cheese, softened at room temperature

1¼ cups sugar

3 large eggs

¼ cup brewed espresso, cooled to room temperature

2 heaping tablespoons all-purpose flour

1 vanilla bean

For the topping

1 (14-ounce) can sweetened condensed milk, label removed

½ cup semi-sweet chocolate chips

Flaky sea salt for sprinkling

1. To make the crust, put a rack in the center of the oven and preheat to 350°F. Grease the inside of an 8- or 9-inch springform pan. Wrap the outside of the pan with aluminum foil (this keeps water from leaking into the cheesecake when you bake it in a bain-marie).
2. Stir the cookie crumbs, melted butter, and sugar together in a medium bowl to combine. Press the crumb mixture to cover the bottom and up the sides of the pan. Bake for 10 minutes and set aside to cool.
3. To make the cheesecake, combine the cream cheese, mascarpone, and sugar in the bowl of a standing mixer fitted with the whisk attachment. Cream on medium-high speed until the mixture is light and fluffy and no lumps remain, stopping to scrape down the sides of the bowl every 2 or 3 minutes. Add the eggs, one at a time, mixing on medium speed after each addition until they all are incorporated. Add the espresso and flour, then mix on medium speed to combine. Split the vanilla bean down the middle with a paring knife and scrape the beans from the pod and into the bowl. Mix on medium speed until all of the ingredients are blended.
4. Put the springform pan in a baking pan and pour water 1 inch up the sides of the pan. Pour the batter into the prebaked crust, smooth the top, and bake for 80 to 90 minutes, until a toothpick inserted into the center comes out clean. (It will jiggle when you shake the pan; it sets as it cools.) Set aside in the bain-marie to cool to room temperature. Remove from the bain-marie, discard the foil, and refrigerate for at least 3 hours.
5. Meanwhile, remove the label from the can of condensed milk and put the can in a saucepan of water. Boil the can for 3 hours, making sure it is submerged at all times. Remove the can and set it aside to allow the dulce de leche to cool for about 10 minutes. It should be room temperature when added to the cheesecake.
6. Run a knife around the edges of the pan to loosen the crust from the sides. Unlatch the pan and carefully remove the sides. Spread half of the dulce de leche over the top, sprinkle the chocolate chips around the edges, and sprinkle with the sea salt. Slice and serve chilled.

New York Vanilla Bean Cheese Cake

I am known among my family, friends, and co-workers for my cheesecake. Being from New York, my mother makes a great cheesecake, so when I started making cheesecake, I used her recipe as a jumping-off point. I add a bit of lemon zest, so the cheesecake is creamy and refreshing instead of just being cheesy. Cheesecake makes a great dessert to bring to a dinner party, because it makes a grand entrance, and everyone loves it. If I am bringing it somewhere, I top the cheesecake with fresh fruit, which makes the cheesecake look so pretty: it's like bringing dessert and flowers at one time. The crust is made from graham cracker crumbs, but if you want to mix things up, you can use any hard cookie, such as gingersnaps, short bread, or chocolate wafer cookies. If you use shortbread cookies, add 2 tablespoons of ground pecans to the mix to keep it from being too buttery and for good texture.

COOK'S TIP: You will need an 8- or 9-inch springform pan to make this dessert.

SERVES 8 TO 10

For the crust

5 tablespoons unsalted butter, melted and cooled to room temperature, plus more cold butter for greasing the pan

2 cups graham cracker crumbs (about 18 rectangular graham crackers)

½ cup sugar

For the cheesecake

2 (8-ounce) packages cream cheese, softened, at room temperature

16 ounces mascarpone or ricotta cheese or sour cream, at room temperature

1½ cups sugar

3 large eggs

2 heaping tablespoons all-purpose flour

1 vanilla bean pod

Finely grated zest of ½ lemon

1. To make the crust, position an oven rack in the center and preheat the oven to 350°F. Grease the inside (bottom and sides) of an 8- or 9-inch springform pan. Wrap the outside of the pan (bottom and sides) with aluminum foil (this keeps water from leaking into the cheesecake when you bake it in a bain-marie).
2. Stir the graham cracker crumbs, melted butter, and sugar together in a medium bowl to combine. Using your hands, press the crumb mixture to cover the bottom and up the sides of the prepared pan. Bake the crust for 10 minutes and set aside to cool to room temperature.
3. To make the cheesecake, combine the cream cheese, mascarpone, and sugar in the bowl of a standing mixer fitted with the whisk attachment. Cream on medium-high speed until the mixture is light and fluffy and no lumps remain, about 8 minutes, stopping to scrape

down the sides of the bowl with a rubber spatula every 2 or 3 minutes. Add the eggs, one at a time, mixing on medium speed after each addition until all of the eggs are incorporated. Turn off the mixer. Add the flour and mix on medium speed just to combine. Split the vanilla bean down the middle with a paring knife. Use the knife to scrape the beans from the pod and into the bowl. Add the lemon zest and mix on medium speed until all of the ingredients are blended.

4. For the bain-marie, put the springform pan in a large baking pan and pour enough water to come 1 inch up the sides of the pan. Pour the batter into the prebaked crust, smooth the top with a rubber spatula, and bake the cheesecake on the middle rack for 80 to 90 minutes, until a toothpick inserted into the center comes out clean. (Note that the cheesecake will still jiggle when you shake the pan; it will set as it cools.) Set the cheesecake aside, still in the bain-marie, to cool to room temperature. Remove the cheesecake from the bain-marie, remove and discard the foil, and refrigerate for at least 3 hours, or ideally, overnight to chill.

5. To remove the cheesecake from the springform pan, run a knife around the edges of the pan to loosen the crust from the sides. Unlatch the pan to release the cake and carefully remove the sides of the pan. Cut the cheesecake into 8 or 10 slices and serve chilled.

LODGE

Skillet Cornbread with Candied Ginger

Last year, I asked my son what he wanted for his birthday and he said he didn't want anything except my cornbread. I baked it in little baby cast iron skillets. They were so cute and he loved them.

I wake up in the middle of the night sometimes thinking "!!!" and just write down whatever it is in my phone. For this dish, I wanted to put something else in it, other than corn. I've seen so many recipes, especially here in California where there's a lot of Mexican and South American influences, I wanted to put something in it that wasn't obvious. I couldn't think of anything, went to sleep, and like a light went on one night I woke, "Candied ginger!" That's how I make it now. It's such an unsuspecting but perfectly fitting flavor.

SERVES 8 TO 10

For the cornbread

¼ cup (½ stick) unsalted butter, melted

1 cup all-purpose flour

1 cup cornmeal

1 teaspoon ground ginger

1 cup sugar

1 teaspoon baking powder

1 teaspoon baking soda

1 teaspoon kosher salt

1 cup whole milk

1 extra-large egg

2 heaping tablespoons mayonnaise

¼ cup chopped candied ginger

½ cup fresh corn kernels (from about 2 ears) or canned or frozen, thawed and drained

For the glaze

¼ cup (½ stick) unsalted butter, melted

2 tablespoons honey

1 pinch kosher salt

1. Preheat the oven to 350°F. Pour the melted butter into a 10-inch cast-iron skillet. Use a pastry brush or paper towel to grease the sides of the pan with the butter.
2. Reserve 1 tablespoon of the flour. In a large bowl, whisk together the remaining flour, the cornmeal, ground ginger, sugar, baking powder, baking soda, and salt. In a small bowl, whisk the milk, egg and mayonnaise together, then pour the wet ingredients into the bowl with the dry ingredients. In a small bowl, toss the candied ginger with the reserved tablespoon of flour and toss to coat. (This prevents the ginger from sinking to the bottom of the pan when the cornbread bakes.) Add the flour-coated ginger and any flour left in the bowl to the batter. Stir in the corn to evenly distribute.
3. Pour the batter into the prepared skillet and bake for 35 to 40 minutes, or until a toothpick inserted into the center comes out clean.
4. Meanwhile, in a small bowl, whisk together the melted butter, honey, and salt to make the glaze.
5. When the cornbread is done, remove it from the oven and use a fork to poke holes all over the surface. Brush the glaze over the cornbread with a pastry brush. (The glaze is best absorbed if you brush it on when the cornbread is hot out of the oven.) Let the cornbread cool slightly. Cut it into wedges and serve.

Sweet Corn Fritters

These started out as traditional savory corn fritters. They are perfect for brunch. A fun treat for my son and his cousin who was staying the night. To make banana-strawberry fritters, which they absolutely love, substitute 1 cup mashed banana and ¼ cup chopped strawberries for the corn in this recipe.

We have fresh corn three quarters of the year—if you can't find it fresh, I would take it frozen as the canned corn is pasteurized and loses a lot of its properties.

MAKES ABOUT 16 FRITTERS OR ENOUGH FOR 6 TO 8 SERVINGS

2 large eggs
½ cup whole milk
1 cup all-purpose flour
¼ cup granulated sugar
1 teaspoon baking powder
1 teaspoon baking soda
1 teaspoon ground cinnamon
½ teaspoon ground nutmeg
½ teaspoon kosher salt
1 cup fresh corn kernels (from about 4 ears) or canned or frozen corn, thawed and drained
Canola or vegetable oil for deep-frying
Confectioners' sugar for dusting

1. Whisk the eggs in a large bowl to break up the yolks then whisk in the milk. In a separate, medium bowl, stir together the flour, granulated sugar, baking powder, baking soda, cinnamon, nutmeg, and salt to thoroughly combine. Add the flour mixture to the bowl with the eggs and milk and stir until no flour is visible. Stir the corn into the batter to evenly distribute.
2. In a medium saucepan, heat 3 to 4 inches of oil until it reaches 350°F. On the counter, make a bed of paper towels.
3. Using a tablespoon, scoop a heaping tablespoon of the batter and use a second tablespoon to push the batter off the spoon and into the oil. Drop as many fritters as will fit in a single layer in the oil without crowding the pan, and fry them until golden brown. (Depending on the size of the pan you're using, you will need to fry two or three batches of fritters.) Using a slotted spoon, transfer the fritters to the paper towels to drain. Use a sift or small metal strainer to dust with confectioners' sugar and fry the remaining batter in the same way. Dust the fritters again right before serving.

Ricotta Biscuits

Before I went to culinary school, baking was not something I did, ever. It was so daunting to me, the way ingredients interacted with one another in the oven. In school, I began to understand the fundamentals of baking, and now I feel much more comfortable doing it than I once did. I even feel comfortable enough to play around with classic recipes, which is what I did with these biscuits. I use ricotta and yogurt in place of buttermilk, which is the standard. Ricotta is such a light, wonderful, fluffy cheese, it works magic in the biscuits. For heartier biscuits, add ¼ cup of ¼-inch cubes of Spanish chorizo, or any sort of meat, to the dough.

MAKES 7 OR 8 BISCUITS

1. Whisk the ricotta, yogurt, milk, and egg together in a large bowl until thoroughly blended.
2. In the bowl of a food processor with a metal blade attachment, pulse the flour, baking powder, and salt to combine. Add the butter and pulse until the mixture resembles coarse meal. Transfer the contents of the food processor to a large bowl. Add the ricotta mixture and mix with a fork until no flour is visible. Bring the dough together into a ball with floured hands, wrap in plastic wrap, and refrigerate for 30 minutes.

½ cup fresh ricotta

¼ cup plain whole milk yogurt

¼ cup whole milk

1 large egg

2¼ cups all-purpose flour, plus more for dusting

2 teaspoons baking powder

1¼ teaspoons kosher salt

¾ cup (1½ sticks) cold unsalted butter, cut into small cubes

1 large egg yolk whisked with 1 tablespoon water to make an egg wash

3. Position an oven rack in the center and preheat the oven to 350°F.

4. Dust a flat work surface or wooden cutting board with flour. Unwrap the chilled dough and place it on the floured work surface. With a floured rolling pin, roll out the dough into a ½-inch-thick rectangle. Fold the sides toward the center in thirds. Return the dough to the refrigerator for 10 minutes and then roll it out again into a ½-inch-thick rectangle. Use a 2- to 3-inch round biscuit or cookie cutter (or a small glass) to cut out 7 or 8 biscuits. Put them on an ungreased baking sheet, leaving 1 inch spaces between them. Brush the tops of the biscuits with the egg wash and bake for 12 to 14 minutes, until the tops are golden brown. Serve warm.

Coconut Custard Pie

This is a dessert that my mom used to make for my sisters and me when we were growing up. I've tweaked it over the years by adding chocolate chips and vanilla. I also add more coconut flakes to the custard than my mom does, because I love coconut more than I love custard. This is the dessert I make most often when I decide to have people for dinner at the last minute and need to throw something together. It's easy to make and the ingredients are always on hand, including store-bought frozen pie crust for just such times.

SERVES 8

3 large eggs

1 cup heavy whipping cream

2 cups (16 ounces) sweet cream of coconut (shake can before opening)

½ cup sugar

1 tablespoon pure vanilla extract

½ cup sweetened coconut flakes

½ cup semi-sweet chocolate chips

Buttery Flakey Everything Dough (page 157), rolled and fitted into a 9-inch pie plate (or 1 frozen store-bought pie crust)

1. Position an oven rack in the center and preheat the oven to 375°F.

2. Whisk the eggs in a large bowl to break up the yolks. Add the cream, coconut cream, sugar, melted butter, and vanilla and whisk to combine. Stir in the coconut flakes.

3. Put the pie shell on a baking sheet. Scatter the chocolate chips over the bottom of the pie shell and pour the filling on top, smoothing the surface with a rubber spatula. Bake on the center rack for 10 minutes. Reduce the heat to 325°F and bake for another 45 to 50 minutes, or until the custard is set. Let cool to room temperature before slicing and serving.

Olive Oil Cranberry Cakes with Candied Oranges

This is definitely one of my favourites. I make a lot of breads and desserts, and people ask me to bake quite often. Olive oil keeps the cake moist and gives it a rich texture.

COOK'S TIP: You will need sixteen 2-inch ramekins to make these little cakes.

MAKES 16 INDIVIDUAL CAKES

For the candied oranges

2½ cups granulated sugar

2 oranges, halved and cut into ⅛-inch-thick slices

For the cakes

1¼ cups all-purpose flour

1 teaspoon baking powder

½ teaspoon baking soda

½ teaspoon kosher salt

2 large eggs

¾ cup granulated sugar

⅓ cup extra-virgin olive oil, plus more for greasing the ramekins

Grated zest of 1 orange plus ⅓ cup fresh orange juice (from 1 orange)

1 teaspoon pure vanilla extract

⅔ cup Mandarin Orange Cranberry Sauce (page 138; or store-bought cranberry sauce)

For the glaze

6 tablespoons unsalted butter, melted

½ teaspoon pure vanilla extract

¾ cup confectioners' sugar

1. Position an oven rack in the center and preheat the oven to 350°F. Grease the ramekins with olive oil and arrange them on a baking tray.
2. To make the candied oranges, line a baking tray with parchment. Sprinkle the parchment paper with ¼ cup of the granulated sugar and set aside.
3. Put the remaining 2¼ cups sugar in a mound in the center of a small saucepan. Pour 6 tablespoons water over the mound, letting it seep into the sugar until it looks like wet sand. Cook this mixture over medium heat without stirring until the sugar has melted and starts to bubble, about 8 minutes. Add the orange slices and simmer until they look glossy and the pulp is translucent. Turn off the heat and use tongs to remove the orange slices, arranging them in a single layer on the sugar-coated baking tray. Set aside.
4. To make the cakes, combine the flour, baking powder, baking soda, and salt in a large bowl and set aside. In the bowl of a standing mixer fitted with a paddle attachment, mix the eggs just to break up the yolks. Add the sugar, olive oil, orange juice, and vanilla, and mix to incorporate. Turn off the mixer, add half of the dry ingredients, and mix on low speed until no flour is visible. Add the remaining dry ingredients and mix on low speed until no flour is visible, then add the cranberry sauce and orange zest, to thoroughly combine.
5. Pour the batter into the prepared ramekins and put the baking tray with the ramekins on the center rack to bake for 12 to 15 minutes, until a toothpick inserted into one of the cakes comes out clean. Set on a wire rack and cool the cakes to room temperature.
6. Meanwhile, make the glaze. Stir the melted butter and vanilla together in a medium bowl. Add the confectioners' sugar and whisk until no lumps remain.
7. When the cakes have cooled, carefully pop them out of the ramekins onto a baking sheet so the bottoms face up. Using the back of a spoon, spread the glaze over the cakes. Decorate with the candied orange slices.

Oatmeal Whole-Wheat Pancakes with Black Cherries

Black cherries are super-sweet and I use them to make a gorgeous barbecue sauce. The season's so short. The darker the color, the better are the cherries for you. That's where all the antioxidants are from. These are my favorite pancakes, and not just because they're (sort of) healthy.

MAKES ABOUT 1 DOZEN PANCAKES

¾ cup quick-cooking rolled oats

½ cup plus 2 tablespoons heavy whipping cream

¾ cup whole-wheat flour

1½ teaspoons kosher salt

1½ teaspoons baking powder

¾ teaspoon baking soda

1 teaspoon ground cinnamon

½ cup whole milk

2 tablespoons unsalted butter, melted and cooled to room temperature, plus more cold butter for cooking the pancakes

1 large egg

1 packed tablespoon light or dark brown sugar

1 teaspoon pure vanilla extract

12 cup pitted and roughly chopped fresh or frozen black cherries (or substitute red cherries, blackberries, or blueberries)

Maple syrup for serving

1. Combine the oats and ½ cup of the cream in a medium bowl and set aside for 10 minutes to soften the oats.
2. Meanwhile, stir together the flour, salt, baking powder, baking soda, and cinnamon in a large bowl to thoroughly combine. Add the milk, melted butter, egg, sugar, and vanilla, and the remaining 2 tablespoons cream. Mix with a spatula until the wet and dry ingredients are combined. Add the softened oats to the bowl and gently fold in the cherries.
3. Heat a griddle or skillet over medium heat. Add some butter and let it melt. Pour the batter into a ¼ cup an pour that onto the griddle. Cook until they are deep golden on both sides, 2 to 3 minutes per side, flipping only once. Serve warm with maple syrup.

Chocolate Chip Cookies with Sea Salt Potato Chips

I love salty and sweet together, so it's not surprising that when someone gave me a dark chocolate-dipped potato chip, I thought it was the best thing I ever tasted. Not long after, I was making chocolate chip cookies to take to a friend's baby shower and I got the idea to throw crumbled potato chips in the cookie dough. The cookies turned out amazing, and now potato chips are a standard addition to my chocolate chip cookies. I like to use very dark, semi-sweet chocolate, going to the market and buying big chunks of it and chopping it up to store in a tin; otherwise I buy packaged chocolate chunks, not chips, for these because big pieces melt into the cookies better.

INGREDIENT NOTE: It's important to use artisanal or natural-type potato chips; something a bit thicker than old-school super-thin potato chips. Crumble them until the pieces are the size of cornflakes.

MAKES ABOUT 4 DOZEN COOKIES

2 cups unsalted butter, softened at room temperature

2 cups packed brown sugar

2 cups granulated sugar

2 large eggs

2 teaspoons pure vanilla extract

2 teaspoons hot water

3 cups all-purpose flour

1½ tablespoons cocoa powder

1 teaspoons baking soda

1 teaspoon fine sea salt or kosher salt

12 ounces bittersweet chocolate, chopped into ½-inch chunks (about 2 cups)

1½ cups crumbled gourmet potato chips (see Ingredient Note)

Flaky sea salt for sprinkling

1. Position one oven rack in the lower third and another in the upper third of the oven. Preheat to 325°F.
2. In the bowl of a standing mixer fitted with the paddle attachment, mix the butter and both sugars on medium-high speed until light and fluffy, about 10 minutes, stopping every few minutes to scrape down the sides of the bowl with a rubber spatula. Add the eggs, vanilla, and hot water, and mix to combine.
3. In a large bowl, stir together the flour, cocoa powder, baking soda, and salt. Add the dry ingredients to the bowl of the mixer and mix on low speed until no flour is visible. Stir in the chocolate chunks and 1 cup of the potato chip crumbles.
4. Scoop heaping tablespoons of the dough (about 1½ inches each) onto an ungreased baking sheet, leaving at least 2 inches between them. Sprinkle a pinch of flaky sea salt and press a few of the remaining potato chip crumbles on each dough ball.
5. Bake for 12 to 14 minutes, until the cookies are golden brown, rotating the baking sheets from front to back and from the upper and lower racks halfway through for even baking. Set the cookies aside to cool slightly before removing them from the baking sheet. Bake the remaining dough in the same way.

Apple Pie

I have very strong opinions about apple pie. I like it very sweet, I add tons of butter—that's what makes it very delicious and brings perfect color to the crust—and the apples should be very soft and gooey, that's how I grew up eating it. Cook the green apples down. They hold their texture, and they're still identifiable. You just let them get bubbly and caramelly—terrific!

SERVES 8

3 to 3½ pounds Granny Smith apples or tart baking apples, peeled, cored, and sliced ¾-inch thick

¾ cup granulated sugar

¾ cup packed light or dark brown sugar

1½ teaspoons ground cinnamon

½ teaspoon freshly grated nutmeg

3 heaping tablespoons all-purpose flour, plus more for dusting

1 recipe Buttery Flakey Everything Dough (page 157), chilled

½ cup (1 stick) cold unsalted butter, cubed

Vanilla ice cream for serving

1. Position an oven rack in the center of the oven and preheat the oven to 400°F.
2. In a large bowl, toss the apples with both sugars, the cinnamon, and nutmeg to coat. Sprinkle the flour over the apples and toss to distribute. Set aside while you make the pie shell.
3. Dust a flat work surface with flour. Remove one disc of the dough (half of the recipe) from the refrigerator and place it on the flour-dusted surface. Dust a rolling pin with flour and roll out the dough into a 12-inch circle. Fold the dough in half, lift it into a 9½-inch pie dish, and unfold it to cover the dish. Using scissors, trim the dough, leaving 1 inch of dough hanging over the edge of the dish. Remove the second disc from the refrigerator and roll it out in the same way. Pour the apple mixture into the prepared pie shell, smoothing it with a rubber spatula to evenly distribute it. Scatter the cubes of butter over the apples. Carefully lift the top crust and center it on top of the pie. Trim the dough using scissors so 1 inch of dough hangs over the edge; fold the excess hanging dough under itself to form a thick rim around the edge of the pie. Using your thumb and index finger, pinch thick mountain peaks around the edges of the pie crust to seal it. Use a small sharp knife to cut a hole or an X in the center of the top crust to allow steam to escape while the pie is baking. Put the pie on a baking sheet and bake it on the center rack until the crust is golden brown, about 1 hour. Set the pie aside to cool slightly before serving. Cut into wedges and serve with ice cream.

Buttery Flaky Everything Dough

This is a standard flaky, buttery pie dough. I add a teaspoon of sugar, which is just enough to bring out the flavor of the butter without making the crust sweet.

MAKES ENOUGH FOR 2 PIE CRUSTS, OR 1 DOUBLE-CRUST PIE

2½ cups all-purpose flour

1 teaspoon granulated sugar

1 teaspoon kosher salt

1 cup (2 sticks) cold, unsalted butter, cut into cubes

¼ cup ice water, or more as needed

1. Combine the flour, sugar, and salt in a large bowl and mix to distribute the sugar and salt.
2. Add the butter and mix it into the flour with your fingertips until the mixture resembles wet crumbs. Add 2 tablespoons of the ice water and continue mixing, adding more water as necessary to bring the dough together into a ball.
3. Divide the ball in half and pat each half to form a disc. Wrap each disc in plastic wrap and refrigerate for at least 1 hour or up to several days. You can wrap any extra dough in plastic wrap and freeze.

Goat Cheese Ice Cream

In culinary school, we had this amazing restaurant-quality ice cream maker, and I got so excited about it, I started using it to make every flavor of ice cream you could imagine. I love good cheese, and especially goat cheese, so during that ice cream-obsessed period of my life, making this was just a natural thing. It's actually light when you taste it, very creamy, and it's not going to get very hard—more like gelato.

COOK'S TIP: This recipe requires an ice cream maker.

SERVES 6 TO 8

4 large egg yolks
1 cup sugar
2 cups heavy whipping cream
½ cup whole milk
4 ounces goat cheese
3 tablespoons light corn syrup

1. Whisk the egg yolks and sugar in a medium bowl until they are pale yellow, 4 to 5 minutes. Set aside.
2. Heat the cream and milk in a medium saucepan over medium heat, stirring constantly, until small bubbles form at the edge, about 5 minutes. Turn off the heat. Gradually add one-quarter of the hot cream mixture to the bowl with the egg yolk mixture to temper the eggs, stirring constantly with a whisk to prevent the hot cream from cooking the eggs. Make a custard by gradually adding the tempered eggs to the saucepan of milk and cream, whisking constantly. Cook the custard over medium-low heat, stirring constantly with a whisk, until it is thick enough to coat the back of a spoon, about 10 minutes. Pass the custard through a fine-mesh strainer into a bowl. Place the bowl over an ice bath until the custard cools completely, about 30 minutes.
3. Meanwhile, combine the goat cheese with the corn syrup in a small mixing bowl. Add a cupful of the custard and whisk the ingredients until no lumps of goat cheese remain. Stir the goat cheese mixture into the bowl of custard. Cover and refrigerate until completely cooled, at least 2 hours or ideally overnight.
4. Pour the ice cream base into an ice cream maker and churn according to the manufacturer's instructions. For the best results, serve straight from the ice cream maker.

Peach Blackberry Buckle

I'm more of a savory than pastry chef, but when I have people for dinner I make everything I serve, It becomes a fruity, doughy, delicious mess, warm and comforting. You just pour the batter into the pan, put the fruit on top, and the oven does the rest. The tops and edges get crispy and golden brown, and the center is soft and heavy with fruit. We have white peaches in LA but I prefer the yellow because they're sweeter and have a stronger flavor. Frozen peaches work as well. Served warm, with vanilla ice cream, this buckle is so impressive, people will think you've been baking all day.

COOK'S TIP: use 8 miniature cast-iron skillets or 4½-inch ramekins, or make a full-size buckle using a deep-dish pie or casserole dish as I have here.

SERVES 8

For the fruit

½ cup (1 stick) unsalted butter

1 cup turbinado (raw) sugar

1 teaspoon kosher salt

2 tablespoons pure vanilla extract

1 teaspoon ground cinnamon

1 teaspoon ground nutmeg

½ bag (5 to 6 ounces) frozen peaches

1 bag (10 to 12 ounces) frozen blackberries

For the batter

1 cup whole-wheat flour

1 cup turbinado (raw) sugar

1 teaspoon baking powder

½ teaspoon kosher salt

1 cup whole milk

½ cup (1 stick) unsalted butter

Vanilla ice cream, for serving

1. Position an oven rack in the center of the oven and preheat the oven to 350°F.
2. To prepare the fruit, combine the butter, sugar, salt, vanilla, cinnamon, and nutmeg in a large saucepan over medium heat and cook until the sugar dissolves. Add the peaches, stir to coat them with the sugar mixture, and cook for 1 minute. Turn off the heat and set aside.
3. To make the batter, in a large bowl, combine the flour, sugar, baking powder and salt, and stir to distribute them evenly. Pour in the milk and mix until the dry ingredients are moistened.
4. Cut the stick of butter into 1-tablespoon segments and put 1 segment in each miniature skillet or ramekin (or put the entire stick of butter in the bottom of a large deep-dish pie or casserole dish). Put the skillets or ramekins on a baking sheet and heat in the oven until the butter begins to bubble, about 10 minutes. If you are using mini skillets, carefully pour the batter to come to just below the rim of each. If you are using ramekins, fill them half full. If you're making one big buckle, pour all of the batter into the large dish.
5. Gently stir the blackberries into the pan with the peaches and spoon the fruit mixture over the batter, dividing it evenly if you are making small buckles. Return the cookie sheet to the oven and bake until golden brown, about 20 minutes for individual buckles; 35 to 40 minutes for a large buckle. Remove the baking sheet from the oven and set aside to cool slightly before serving. Serve warm with vanilla ice cream.

Donuts with Pomegranate Caramel

A couple of years ago, I took my son, Knight, to visit a friend's church and they were offering coffee and donuts afterward. Knight was such a little guy that I didn't even know he knew the word "donut" and suddenly he was like, "I need more donut!" I feel that way about donuts myself. I don't want them anywhere near me when I know I have to perform because I have absolutely no self control over donuts. I make these when Knight and I want to indulge our cravings. I put a bourbon-based pomegranate glaze on them, but he likes a plain glaze; he's a classic kind of guy.

MAKES 10 TO 12 DONUTS

3 (¼-ounce) packages rapid-rise yeast

½ cup hot water

7½ cups all-purpose flour, plus more for dusting

¾ cup sugar

1½ teaspoons kosher salt

½ cup vegetable shortening

2½ cups boiling water

3 large eggs

Canola oil or vegetable oil for deep-frying

1 recipe Pomegranate Caramel (page 164)

1. Combine the yeast and the hot water in the bowl of a standing mixer fitted with a paddle attachment and set aside for 5 minutes to activate the yeast. Add 3 cups of the flour, the sugar, and salt, and mix on low speed to combine, then add the shortening and mix to combine. Add the eggs one at a time, scraping the bowl with a rubber spatula after each addition. Tip in the boiling water and blend well. Add the remaining flour and mix to combine. Increase the speed to medium and mix for 2 minutes, until the dough is smooth and no longer sticks to the side of the bowl.
2. Take the bowl off the stand. Cover it with a kitchen towel or paper towel and set aside in a warm place for 1 hour, until the dough has risen to about double its size.
3. Lightly dust a flat work surface and your rolling pin with flour. Turn the dough out onto the work surface and roll it out until it is ½ inch thick. Cut out 10 to 12 donuts with a donut cutter or a 2- to 3-inch biscuit cutter. Place them on a baking sheet, cover them with the kitchen towel, and set aside in a warm place to rise for 45 minutes.
4. In a medium saucepan, heat 2 to 3 inches of oil over medium heat until it reaches 350°F. Prepare a bed of paper towels for draining.
5. Drop the donuts into the oil and fry until golden brown, 45 seconds to 1 minute per side. Remove the donuts from the oil and drain them on the paper towels. Drizzle them with the pomegranate glaze and serve warm. If not serving immediately, drizzle over some more glaze once you are about to serve.

Pomegranate Caramel

I love pomegranate seeds for the color and the flavor, and we grew up eating them—they were like little jewels. I use this two ways: as a donut glaze and also, without the butter, as a syrup for duck (see Peking Duck, page 103) or to drizzle on pancakes. But they're a lot of work for such a little thing! They have a distinctive flavor and go great with the donuts.

MAKES ABOUT 1½ CUPS

1½ cups pomegranate seeds

4 allspice berries

4 whole cloves

1 cinnamon stick

1 packed cup light or dark brown sugar

1½ cups bourbon

¼ teaspoon cayenne pepper

½ cup (1 stick) unsalted butter, cut into cubes (use if making a glaze)

1. Combine the pomegranate seeds and ½ cup water in a small saucepan and bring to a boil over high heat.
2. Add the allspice, cloves, cinnamon stick, and brown sugar. Return the liquid to a boil. Reduce the heat and simmer until the seeds are mushy and nearly all of the liquid has evaporated, about 10 minutes. Pour through a fine-mesh strainer into a medium bowl; discard the contents of the strainer and return the syrup to the saucepan.
3. Add the bourbon and bring the mixture to a boil over high heat. Reduce the heat and simmer until thick and syrupy. Turn off the heat and stir in the cayenne to finish the syrup. If you are creating a glaze, add the butter and stir until it is thoroughly incorporated. Any remainder glaze can be stored in the refrigerator.

Pumpkin Mascarpone Spanakopita

This breakfast pastry is made with phyllo dough, which you can buy frozen. It's so easy to work with, which makes this spanakopita really simple to put together, and yet it's such a special treat to serve to friends. I'm so into pumpkin—from bread to muffins, pancakes to soup, and we have a great choice from September through to March here in LA.

SERVES 8

1 (2-pound) butternut squash, halved lengthwise, seeds removed

½ cup (1 stick) plus 2 tablespoons unsalted butter, melted

10 ounces mascarpone cheese, softened at room temperature

¾ cup turbinado (raw) sugar

1 teaspoon ground cinnamon

¼ teaspoon ground cloves

1 vanilla bean pod

All-purpose flour for dusting

1 (1-pound) package frozen phyllo dough, thawed according to package instructions

1 large egg whisked with 1 tablespoon water to make an egg wash

1. Position an oven rack in the center of the oven and preheat the oven to 375°F.
2. Put the squash on a baking tray, cut sides up. Using a pastry brush, paint the cut sides with 2 tablespoons of the butter and sprinkle lightly with salt. Bake on the center rack until the squash is tender, 45 to 55 minutes. Set aside to cool slightly. Scoop the squash flesh out of the peel and into a large bowl; discard the peel. Mash the squash with a potato masher. Add the mascarpone, sugar, cinnamon and cloves. Scrape the vanilla beans out of the pod and into the bowl. (Save the pod for another use; boil it in water for the world's best air freshener or put it in a jar of sugar to make vanilla sugar.) Mash the squash filling together until the ingredients are thoroughly combined and the filling is smooth.
3. Dust a flat work surface with flour and lay out one sheet of the phyllo on it. Brush the phyllo with some of the remaining ½ cup of melted butter and lay another sheet of dough on top of it. Brush with more butter and continue in this way until you have stacked 10 sheets of dough. Spread half of the squash mixture over the surface of the dough, leaving bare a 1½-inch border around the edges of the dough. Starting at a short edge, roll the dough up like a scroll. Lift it onto one half of an ungreased baking sheet. Repeat, making another spanakopita roll using the 10 additional sheets of phyllo and the remaining squash mixture. Put the second roll on the baking sheet with the first one. Brush the outsides of both rolls with the egg wash.
4. Bake the spanakopita on the center rack until it is golden brown and crispy, 40 to 45 minutes. Remove from the oven and set aside to cool for about 5 minutes before slicing. Cut each spanakopita into 2-inch-wide slices and serve warm.

Cocktails

Coquito

This is my culture's version of egg nog, made with a mixture of sweetened condensed milk, evaporated milk, and coconut milk. You can buy it, but like egg nog, it's one of those things that's pretty much only around during the holiday season. It was something I was not allowed to drink as a kid because it's high in rum, but I always remember it being part of the tradition.

INGREDIENT NOTE: Make sure you have true cinnamon (*Cinnomomum Zeylanicum*) rather than Cassia cinnamon (*Cinnamomum Cassia*) because it has better flavor and is healthier for you

SERVES 4

2 cups fresh coconut milk or 1 (15-ounce) can coconut milk

1 (14-ounce) can condensed milk

1 (12-ounce) can evaporated milk

2 egg yolks

Pinch of salt

¼ teaspoon Ceylon cinnamon (sold as Mexican cinnamon or canela in Hispanic markets)

1 cup Puerto Rican white rum

Ground cinnamon

1. Place everything except the ground cinnamon in a blender and process for 3 minutes on high speed until the liquid is frothy. Serve chilled in tumblers, dusted lightly with a little cinnamon.

Kelis's Sangria

Sangria feels like summer to me and everyone drank it like water when I was living in Spain. I serve it all the time when I entertain at home. It's refreshing, delicious, and it looks really pretty in a big jug. Also it's perfect for a summer barbecue or a picnic. You can make a red version with strawberries, black grapes, and oranges, or a white one with white wine and thick slices of citrus fruits. I like entertaining so it's fun to be able to serve a good sangria.

SERVES 4 TO 6

1 (750-ml) bottle red wine (choose a mid-price Spanish red wine)

½ (750-ml) bottle high-quality tequila or rum

2 cups sugar

1 tablespoon pure vanilla extract

1 teaspoon ground nutmeg

1 teaspoon ground cinnamon

A handful of mint sprigs

Fresh cherries, grapes, sliced apples, and orange wedges

1 (750-ml) bottle chilled sparkling mineral water

1. In a large pot, combine the wine, tequila, sugar, vanilla, nutmeg and cinnamon. Stir until the sugar has dissolved. Add the mint sprigs and fruit, cover, and refrigerate for 1 to 2 hours to marinate the fruit. Just before serving, add the mineral water and transfer to a glass jug.

COLUMBIA

Index

It takes an army of extremely focused and skilled people to put together a project like this. We were on deadline, and this is my first book so there was so much to learn and so little time.

I want to say thank you to my husband for a million reasons but mostly because on the worst days you always tell me I'm good enough. Thank you, Knight, for your relentless honesty even when I don't ask if you liked it. I should say thank you to my sister Bean because you were officially my first taste tester when we were just little girls. I'd like to point out that you survived.

I need to say thank you, Steve. When I told you food was next for me you didn't run. You trusted me and you stood behind me and made this all happen. You're family now, man. Thank you, Geoff, for your undying diplomacy and willingness to laugh even in the 11th hour when anyone else would throw in the towel.

Thank you, Alexis, for putting up with me in every situation and always pointing out that we could eat churros. Thank you, Brittany, for being my sous chef before you had any idea what that meant or why this was happening to you.

To Kyle, thank you for taking a chance on me, this has meant the world to me: it's my biography on plates. And I'm so happy! Thank you, David, for your impeccable eye for delicious. You are legendary and it was such an honor to have you in my home and a part of this love project with me. Thank you, Anita, for your amazing design. Thank you to Hannah for your attention to detail and your always beautiful artwork. Thank you, Robin, for bringing the finest bits to me. It was like playing dress up. Sophia, Sarah, and Jessica, thank you for your kitchen collaborations, getting the food in front of the camera, and making sure it was always beautiful in the process. Carolynn, thanks for your help bringing this book to life. Thank you, as always, Maisha, for making my hair as big as possible and Gaby, for make up. Thank you to Bronwyn and the Spice Station for always being hospitable and for being one of my favorite places to shop with or without the cameras!

Mom, I can't say thank you enough. But thank you.